NORTHERN ITALY

The World in Color

NORTHERN ITALY

MATHIEU SMEDTS

Photographs by
KEES SCHERER

translated by J. R. Foster

FOLLETT PUBLISHING COMPANY
Chicago - New York

The paperback edition is sold subject to the condition that it shall not, by way of trade or otherwise, be lent, re-sold, hired out, or otherwise circulated without the publisher's prior consent in any form of binding or cover other than that in which it is published and without a similar condition including this condition being imposed on the subsequent purchaser.

First published in Great Britain in 1967
© 1967 C.I.B. The Hague, Holland
English translation by Joe Foster
© 1967 Methuen & Co. Ltd.
Printed in Holland
Library of Congress Catalog Card number 67 17284
Follett Publishing Company
1010 West Washington Boulevard
Chicago, Illinois 60607
6406

Lay-out: D. Ludwig

CONTENTS

Introduction   page   7

A Short History   25

Town and Country   57

The People   89

The Traveller   99

INTRODUCTION

To a confirmed traveller with an interest in the countries he visits few things are more interesting — when he is not actually travelling — than reading guide books. How splendid the old ones were, the exhaustive sort, which told the traveller everything he could possibly want to know about the country to which he was going. The visit to a town usually began at the station. One started out from there with the thick book in one's hand.
Things have changed a good deal in the course of time, but people still want to know something about the countries they visit and the people who live there. It is amusing to note that one no longer needs to take any gold coins! On the whole, it is now much easier than it was once to obtain enlightenment about a country, a province or a city. Anyone who wants to go to Italy can obtain information all over the place, either in his own country or in Italy itself. In Italy people everywhere are ready to help you, and the government spends large sums to ensure that the tourist receives as good a welcome as possible and that all his needs are met for his stay to be as pleasant as it can be.

So far as Northern Italy is concerned there is only one difficulty: there is so much to see that it is difficult to sum it all up in a few pages of text and a number of photographs. Both photographer and writer have had to make a choice, and both are convinced that it is the best choice that could be made from the abundant material available. The young tourist, to whom I have written a letter of advice in the last chapter, may perhaps say when he returns from his travels as the Queen of Sheba did after her visit to Solomon: "I was not told the half". I should agree with him. Everyone discovers his own Italy, his own treasures; Northern Italy is inexhaustible, as anyone who has ever been in Milan, Venice, Siena or Spoleto will agree.

That is just it — anyone who has once visited Northern Italy will return to his own country with his own discoveries, which will be continually extended on subsequent visits, and however splendid the photographs, however carefully considered the text of a book such as this one, he will soon be able to say, when he has feasted his eyes on the reality: "there was more." We ourselves, the photographer and the author, have repeatedly made the same discovery. Every time we visit Northern Italy again we make fresh discoveries.

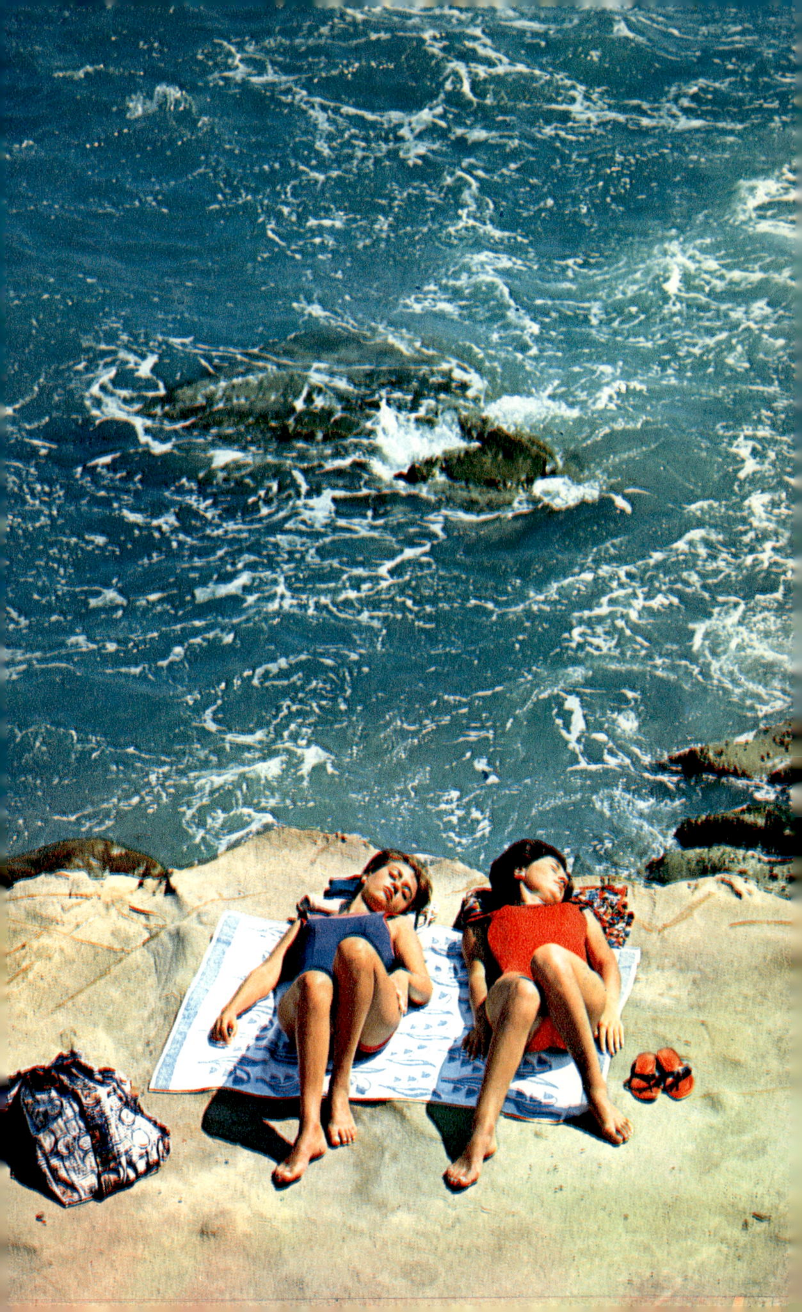

2. Hotel in Diano Marina
◀ 1. Diano Marina

3. Camogli

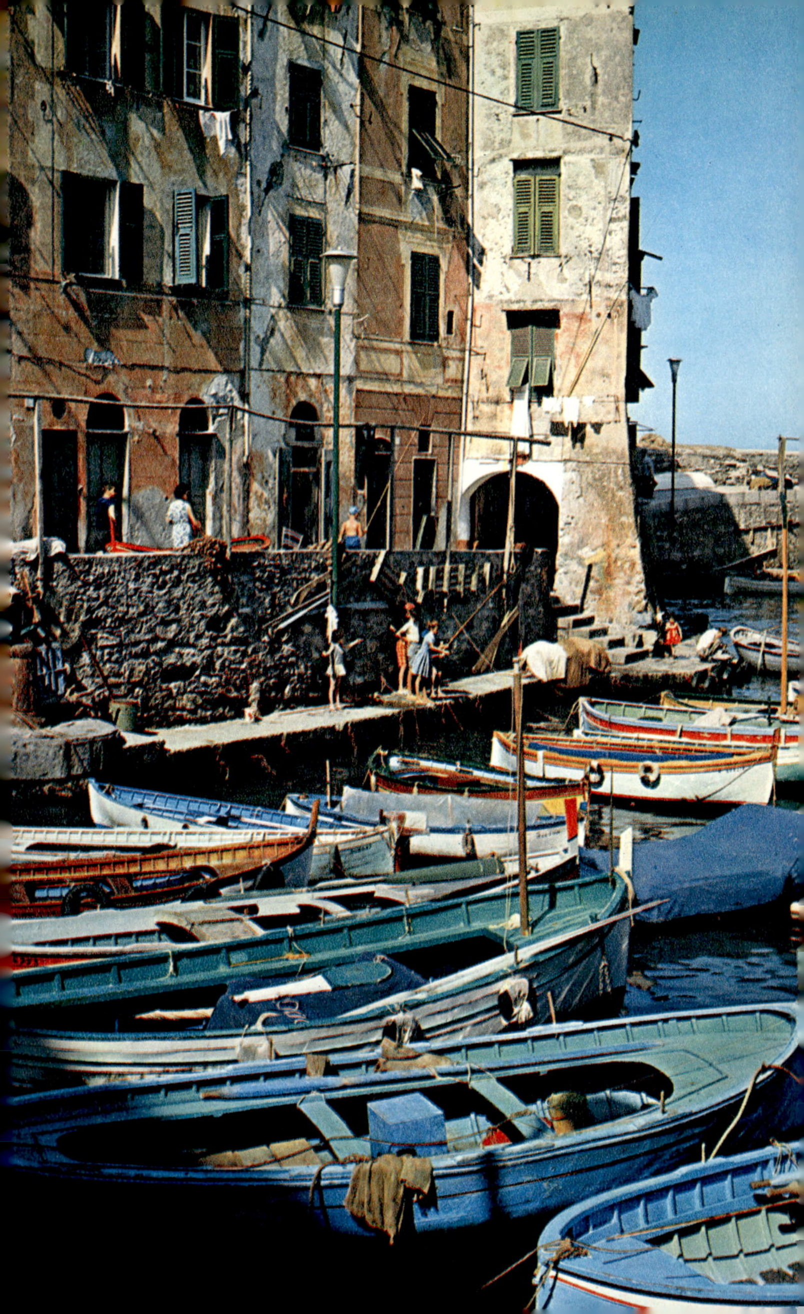

5. Alassio
◀ 4. Camogli

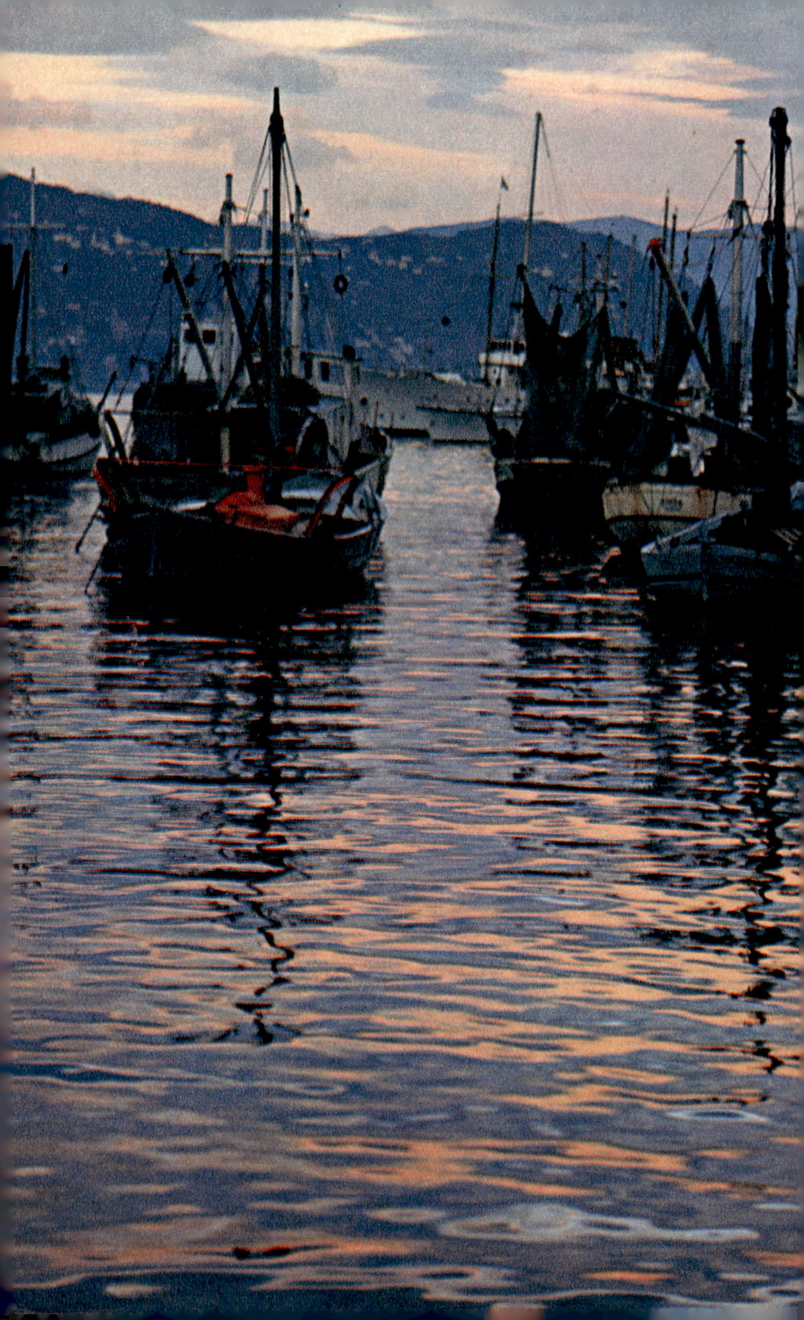

6 / 7. Santa Margherita Ligure

8. Camogli

9. Portofino

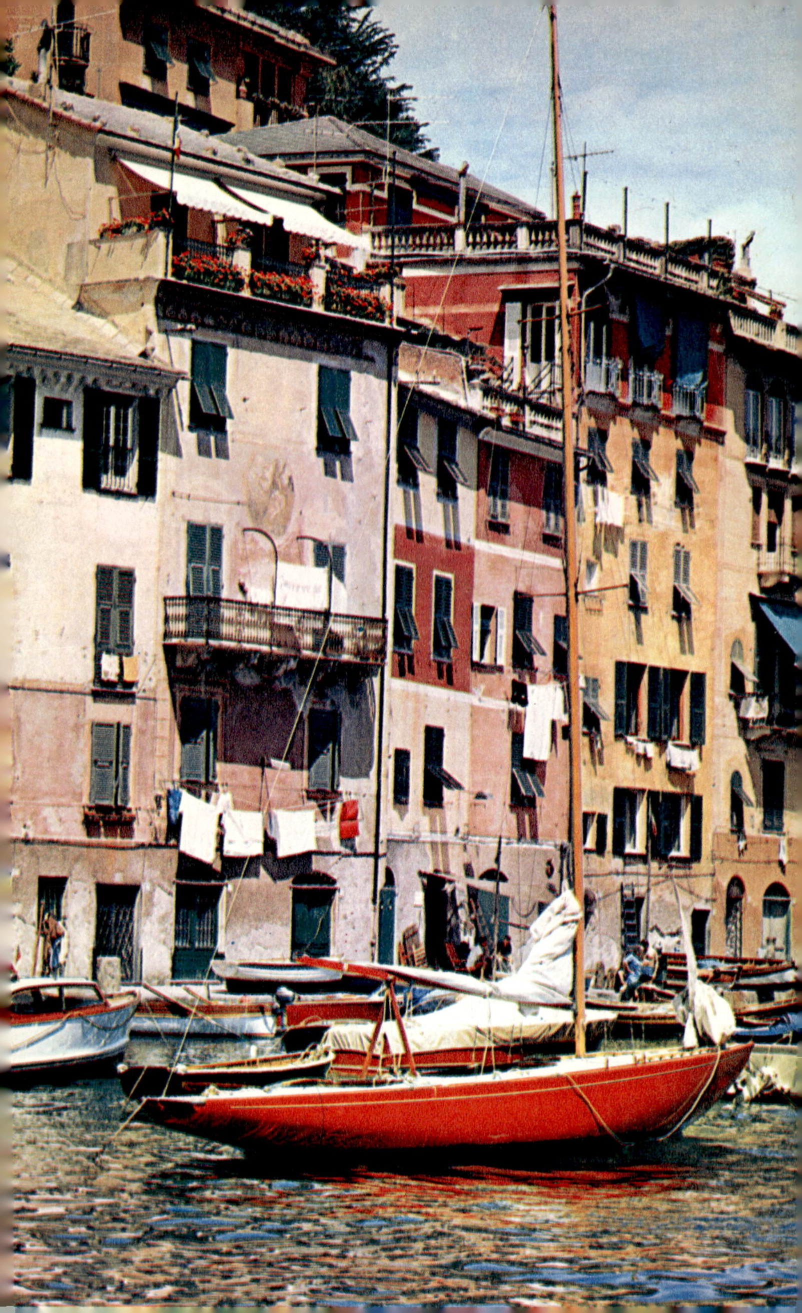

11. San Remo (»taxi«)
◀ 10. Portofino

12. Rapallo

13. Camogli

14. Santa Margherita Ligure

15. Genoa, Porto di San Andrea

16. Bordighera

A SHORT HISTORY

"Italy is a dainty morsel." This is a saying of the notorious Caesar Borgia, son of Pope Alexander VI, who dreamed of a powerful, united Italy. In it he indicated one of the reasons for the sometimes famous but frequently disastrous history of the country and for its divided state. There have always been men — and Caesar was one of them — who wanted to bite off a piece of it for themselves. In his time — the end of the fifteenth century and the beginning of the sixteenth — the country was rich, perhaps richer than it has ever been, except for the kingdom of Naples in the south (a region that has remained poor right down the centuries; it is only in the last few years that the poverty prevailing there has begun to grow somewhat less severe). At that time the civilization of the Renaissance, the rebirth of Greek and Roman culture, had reached its zenith in central and northern Italy. But it was a fragmented country. Poets like Petrarch and Dante sang the blessing of the unity that had existed in the time of the Romans. Caesar Borgia was all for political unity, so long as it was he who brought it about.

His misdeeds have frequently been described in detail. He was a child of his age, with all its virtues and vices in their most extreme form. He commanded the papal army at a moment in the history of the papacy when, as its admirer Machiavelli was to say, it was without spiritual authority and had gone astray by seeking temporal power. The struggle was remorseless and no ruler shrank from political murders. The four other big Italian states were no better, although Caesar Borgia temporarily had more success. The Duchy of Milan, ruled by the Sforzas, was, like the republics of Florence and Venice, — and Rome, too, of course — a centre of artistic life. The same is true, to a smaller degree, of the kingdom of Naples.

These five states were always ready to take up arms against each other, usually with the help of foreign allies, who who had their own designs on the "dainty morsel". Thus in the sixteenth century Italy became the pawn of Europe and twelve wars were fought over it. At the Congress of Vienna in 1815, held after the fall of Napoleon, Count von Metternich, the Austrian Minister for Foreign Affairs, could declare that Italy was not a country, but only "a geographical expression", which for him was afterwards a reason or excuse for seeking to perpetuate this tiresome situation with all the means at his disposal.

It is therefore difficult to talk about the history of Northern Italy. Each place has its own history and is proud of it. Venice, which first arose when the Roman Empire came to an end, ruled the Adriatic coast and stretches of the interior, as far as Verona; the city-state preserved its independence until the time of Napoleon. The mighty castles of Mantua, Faenza, Ferrara and Milan bear witness to the days when these cities were independent and obstinately defending this independence, while frequently trying at the same time to conquer the territory of their neighbours.

The weak, the inhabitants of the small towns and villages, who always had to foot the bill, sometimes grew tired of the situation and banded together in a little confederacy. A good example of this is the League of Seven Countries,

Etruscan vase

founded in 1310. It consisted of seven small towns and villages in the mountainous country to the north of Vicenza: Asiago, Roana, Rotzo, Gallio, Enego, Foza and Lusiano. These sturdy mountaineers had had enough of the plundering carried out by groups of passing mercenaries who had not received any pay. When they went out to till their land they took their arms with them; they even took them to church on Sundays. The priest would count the weapons left in the porch to see if all his beloved parishioners were present. The League had ambassadors in Vicenza, Verona, Florence and Vienna, and remained independent up to the treaty of Campo Formio in 1807, when, like most of Italy, it had to bow before Napoleon.

The golden age lasted for three centuries, the fourteenth, fifteenth and sixteenth. Trade brought wealth. Through it, and through industry, many small places which had languished ever since the Roman period attained a new lease of bustling life. The traces left by these years are to be seen all over northern Italy.

Machiavelli, the Florentine statesman (1469—1527), the pioneer of Italian unity, was one of the few who saw the dangers of the continual warfare, but his warnings went unheeded. He died in the year in which Rome was pillaged by the troops of the Emperor Charles V, a deed which Charles regretted to the day of his death at San Juste in Spain (1559). Three years after the sack of Rome Florence fell; the city had called on the French for help and then had to accept the rule of Spain (1530). That year marked the beginning of a long period of decline for Italy. It was not the first time that this had happened. Frequently in histories of the country one meets the sentence: "Then began a long period of anarchy and decline."

That was why the armies of Napoleon were able to occupy the country without difficulty in the early years of the nineteenth century. Even Venice fell, a city which, under the rule of the Doges, had always been able to keep its independence, even when the Mediterranean had ceased to be *the* world sea as a result of the rise of countries — England, Spain, Holland — washed by other seas. The Doges used to conclude a symbolic marriage with the sea, as a symbol of gratitude to the source of the city's wealth and power. When Venice wanted to resist Napoleon, the latter, who was familiar with its history, said that the Doge would have to take care that he was not compelled to consummate this marriage with himself, Napoleon. The French dictator came and the Doge fell. Later on, under Metternich's leadership, the diplomats of the Congress of Vienna hastened to restore the old situation. Austria annexed the Duchy of Milan and Venice. Hapsburg princes and princesses ruled over little states like Modena, Parma and Tuscany. The Pope regained his Papal States, which were ruled with a firm hand but usually not in the interests of the inhabitants. The whole of southern Italy came under Ferdinand I, king of the two Sicilies, a ruler of Spanish origin. There was only one monarch who, if one did not

Perugia: Palazzo dei Priori (detail)

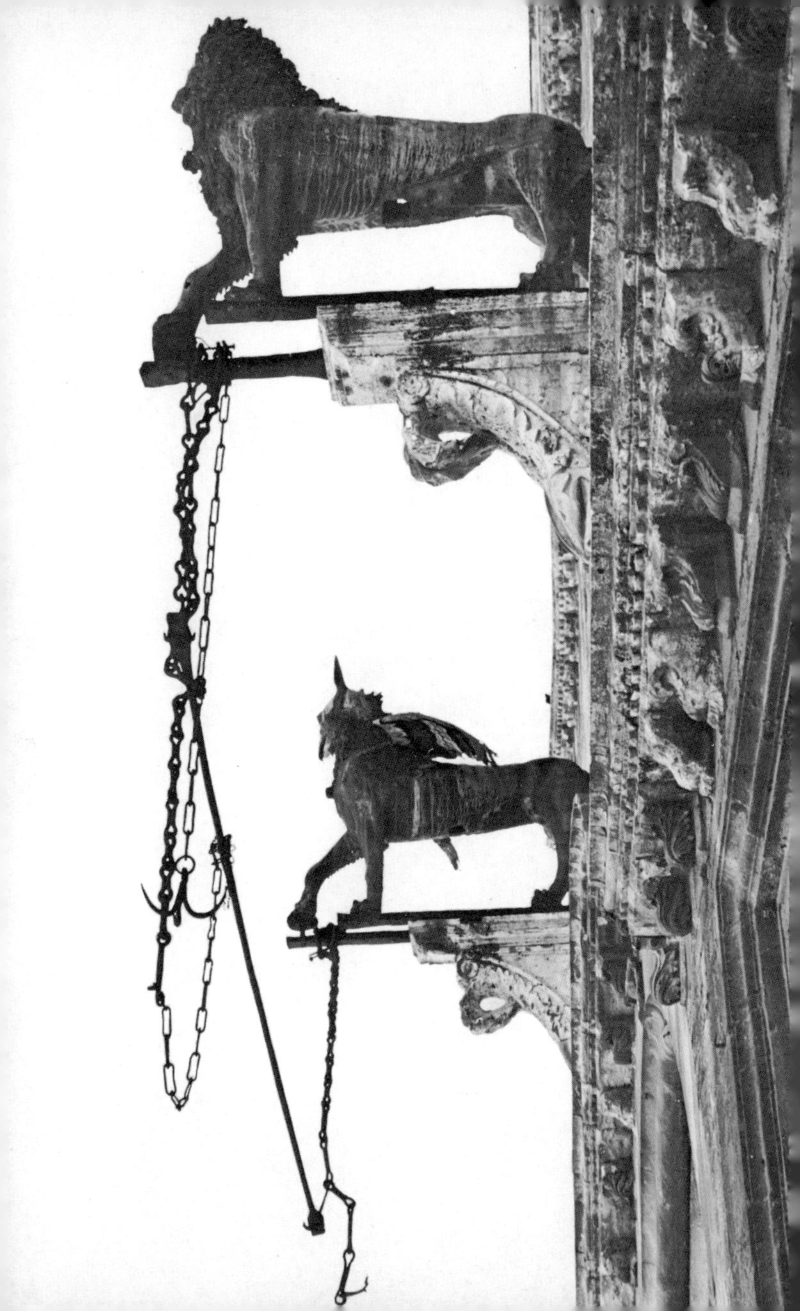

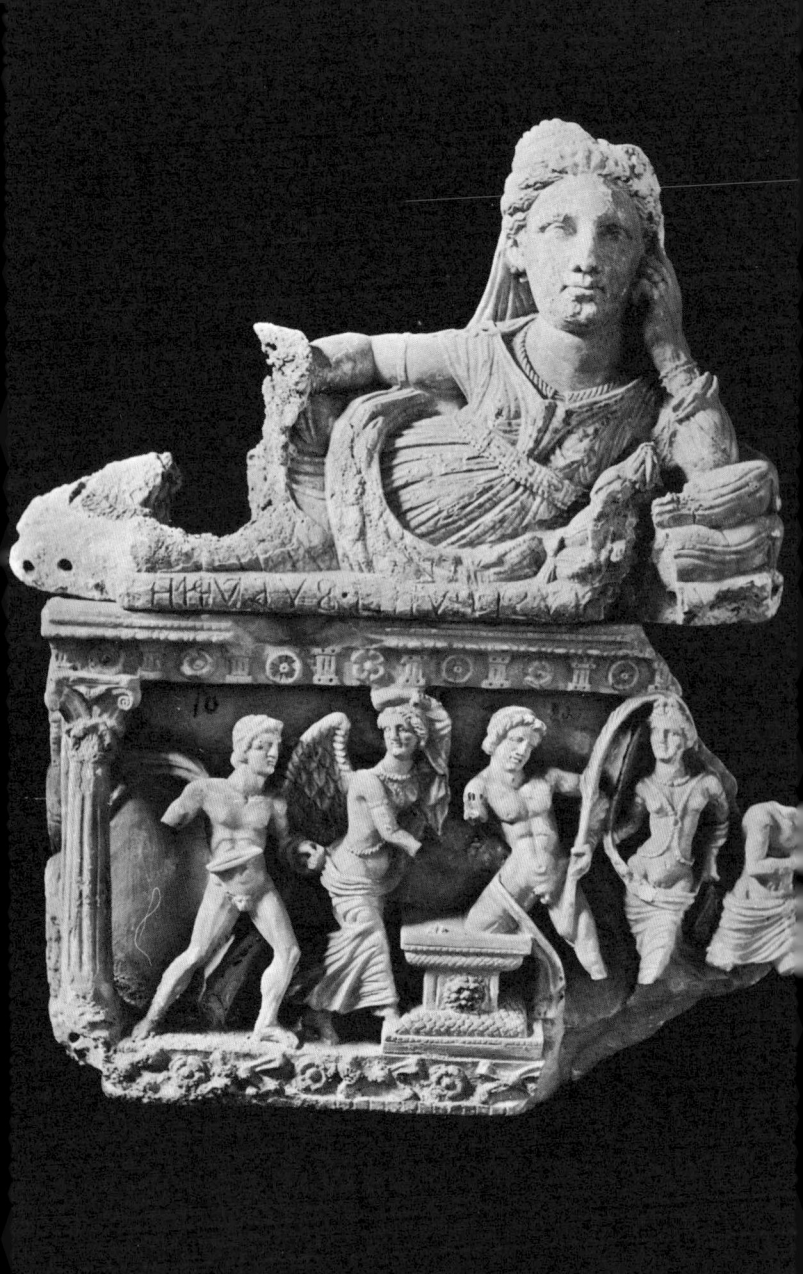

peer too closely, was really Italian, or at any rate whose interests lay in Italy alone, and that was Victor Emmanuel I, the King of Sardinia.

During the period of French supremacy the yearning for unity had grown strong, especially among the intellectuals. But the chances of attaining unity had seldom been so slender as after the Congress of Vienna. The secret police were hard at work. A famous book of this period is Silvio Pellico's *Le Mie Prigioni*, (My Imprisonments; 1832). As leader of an underground movement called 'The Charcoal Burners' he was arrested by the Austrians and spent ten years in gaol.

Strong, self-governing cities have always been a charecteristic of Italy. What happened in the fourteenth and fifteenth centuries, when the power of the Papacy was broken and the cities made themselves independent, was nothing new. In the seventh and sixth centuries before Christ the Etruscans, who lived in central Italy between the Tiber and the Arno, formed a federation of twelve autonomous cities. Among the Greeks in southern Italy and Sicily the city was the basis of the political and commercial system. In due course the Romans defeated the Etruscans and subjugated the country, but it was not until the reign of the Emperor Hadrian (117 - 138 A.D.) that a strong central government was finally established. Afterwards the Roman power spread out swiftly over the world, to far beyond the frontiers of Italy, along the shores of the whole Mediterranean and away to the north, "to the end of the earth", as a monk wrote in the eighth century with more enthusiasm than accuracy. For him the end was England. Italy became a daintier morsel than ever. On the northern frontier in particular strong barbarian tribes — Germanic tribes like the Heruli, the Visigoths and the Vandals — stood quivering to bite a piece of it off. Italy, and this meant in the first place northern Italy, lay more and more open to attacks from outside. In 330 the seat of government of the Roman Empire was transferred to Byzantium. Veterans who had rendered loyal service in the legions were given land on

Urn from an Etruscan grave

Venice — like Rome, a city of cats

the frontiers. They were at the same time both farmers and soldiers. This had already happened in more prosperous times. For example, in the pre-Christian era Aquileia, between Trieste and Venice, had been founded as a colony of veterans, but in those days such settlement had been springboards for further conquests; in the decline of the Empire their purpose was defence against the barbarian pressure.

Emperor Augustus (27 B.C. - 14 A.D.) had his headquarters in Aquileia during his war against the Germans. It is clear from the excavations how important the quiet town of today was at that time. There is a Roman triumphal way and the remains of a harbour by a splendid avenue of cypresses and now the floors and walls of big Roman houses are gradually coming to light in the meadows. There is a beautifully arranged museum, where one can see the little golden flies from the head-veils of the Roman ladies of those days — a fashion that is now very modern again! There are also early Christian remains, such as the mosaic floors in the splendid basilica.

Aquileia is one of the quiet little places in northern Italy that have a long history and, as the guide-books say, are worth a detour. Ravenna is better known. It was the city where, in 49 B.C., Julius Caesar decided not to obey the command of the Roman Senate and discharge his troops, but instead to cross the Rubicon, the boundary between Italy and Gallia Cisalpina. "Let the die be cast," Caesar is supposed to have said. So began the civil war, which in the view of some historians was the beginning of the Roman Empire. A good four centuries later the Emperor

Honorius established his headquarters in Ravenna, and this marked the beginning of the end of the same empire. The town lay amid swamps and was built on piles; it thus provided a secure refuge when the attacks of the barbarians became fiercer. The Romans had by then become Christians. The Emperor Constantine the Great (306 - 337) hoped with the help of Christ to be able to hold off the foe. Some of the mosaics at Ravenna bear witness to this. In one of them Jesus is depicted as a young Roman soldier, beardless, in a short tunic, a figure very different from the bearded Byzantine Christ with which we have subsequently become familiar.

Rome's conversion was of no avail. In 476 the last Roman emperor was deposed and was succeeded by a general, Odoacer, a Rugian in the service of Rome. The dark ages had begun. In the next century Byzantium conquered part of Italy. Then the Lombards, who were to give their name to Lombardy, pressed into the north, while in central Italy the popes established the Papal States. Later on the Franks entered northern Italy. In 774 Charlemagne took the pope under his protection. In the south Byzantium was still able to maintain its power, but the partition of Italy was now an accomplished fact. There are more remains from the time of the Roman Empire than from the turbulent centuries after its fall. And the finest relics of these centuries are to be found in Ravenna, namely, the incredibly beautiful mosaics in the churches and in the mausoleum of Gallia Placidia, the sister of the Emperor Honorius. It is strange to think that for two centuries this busy little provincial town was the centre of European civilization. Afterwards it never played any significant part in history, although many battles raged in its vicinity, the last of them in the Second World War. Once in one of these restless periods Dante found a welcome there, after being banished from his native city of Florence. It was there that he saw his Beatrice and wrote part of his *Divine Comedy.* His grave attracts many visitors.

At one point, towards the end of the eighth century, it

looked as if stability would return. In 774 Charlemagne had crowned himself in Pavia with the iron crown of the Lombard kings, and Pope Leo III crowned him Roman emperor. Peace reigned for a time. The farmers of the Po valley were able to till their fruitful land undisturbed. This region was the country's granary, and it therefore attracted invaders, who soon appeared again after Charlemagne's death, when it became evident that his sons were incapable of keeping his empire together. Even the Hungarians penetrated into northern Italy. In 951 the German, Otto the Great, came to have himself crowned emperor in his turn in Rome. That was the beginning of a conflict between the popes and the emperors over the right to name those who were to hold high office in the Church — the struggle over Investitures. Up to the death of the Emperor Henry III in 1065 the popes were on the losing side; after that it became clearer and clearer that the emperors were not in a strong position to keep both Germany and Italy itself under their thumbs. The Italian cities, which always had to foot the bill and were continually pillaged, thankfully grasped the chance to develop independently. They built strong walls and became autonomous. Venice, founded by people who had taken refuge on the islands in the lagoons at the time of the Hun invasions, now became a powerful commercial city which hired out its fleets to carry the crusaders to the East. Milan and Genoa, Lucca and Pisa, Siena and Florence now began to flourish; they were in fierce competition with each other and often came to blows. Even the good Francis of Assisi (1182 - 1226) took part, in his light-hearted youth before his conversion, in many a battle against other cities.

In 1176 the cities of Lombardy, which had joined together in a league, defeated the Emperor Frederick Barbarossa; their autonomy was recognized in the Peace of Constance (1183). Not only did the cities fight against each other; the inhabitants of each single city were often at each other's throats. It was the time of the Guelfs and Ghibelines. The former were the retainers of the popes; the Ghibelines supported the claims of the emperor. In Florence the Guelfs were also divided among themselves, so that Dante, who belonged to the white Guelfs and was against the temporal power of the popes, did not hesitate, in his *Divine Comedy*, to consign the pope to hell. In many cities, such as Bologna, Pavia and San Gimignano, the rich families build strong towers from which to fight each other. A number of them have survived, monuments to the love of strife, symbols of the divided character of the period.

People could allow themselves the luxury of this swaggering behaviour. Trade and industry flourished. Italian wool dealers competed with the Flemish ones in the English market. Explorers like Marco Polo made long journeys, as far as China, whence he brought back spaghetti with him. The cities also competed in the realm of art. The civilisation of the Renaissance, which flowered in the fourteenth and fifteenth centuries, came into existence because the despots, who frequently came to power by cruel means, wanted to make their cities into living museums. They were even ready to fight for artists, who were thus enabled to make a living out of them, like Leonardo da Vinci, who worked for seventeen years, from 1482 to 1499, at the court of the Sforzas at Milan. The artists' work had to be grandiose, for the rulers wished to show rival cities how rich and powerful they were. Listen to the proclamation announcing the construction of Florence cathedral: "To the honour of the municipality and people of Florence a building shall arise of such great and exceptional splendour that nothing greater or more beautiful could be achieved by human industry." The project was intended to make a lasting impression on Florence's neighbour at Pisa and Lucca, a conception warmly applauded by the great Lorenzo de Medici, 'il Magnifico' (1449-1492), who was to complete the proud building, begun in 1296. Make an impression on the others! The builders of St. Mark's at Venice, and of the cathedrals of Pisa and Milan, had the same idea in mind.

This period has therefore left a strong stamp on Italian cities.

The bitter enmities and envy were bound to be fatal to the

country in the end. As we have already mentioned, poets like Dante and Petrarch and a sober realist like Machiavelli foresaw this, but they were voices crying in the wilderness, even if the wilderness was a splendid one. It is rather surprising that the country did not become a real wilderness, for from the end of the fifteenth century onwards wars were continually being fought out by foreign armies in Italy, especially northern Italy. Italy's history was part of the history of other countries, and it is amazing that Italy itself suffered so little devastation; but the walls of the castles and cities were thick and the artillery used stone projectiles. With the arrival of the Reformation and of the Catholic Church's reply to Luther, the Counter-Reformation, the influence of the Renaissance began to decline. Even before the end (in 1563) of the Council of Trent, at which many points

Florence: Ponte Vecchio

of Catholic doctrine were formulated more strictly, the intellectual freedom which had flourished under the Renaissance popes was restricted. The Inquisition had appeared upon the scene, as Giordano Bruno (1548-1600) among others discovered. He was a champion of Christian freedom, and after years of wandering about Europe he died at the stake in Rome. Galileo (1564-1642) had to renounce the teaching of Copernicus that the earth goes round the sun. By the treaty of Cateau-Cambrésis (1559) Spain gained the upper hand in Italy. This was a thorn in the flesh of Louis XIV of France, but he was defeated in the War of the Spanish Succession; however, this did not help Italy, for by the Treaty of Utrecht (1713) Spanish rule was replaced by Austrian rule. In 1748 the war over the Austrian Succession came to an end with the Peace of Aix-la-Chapelle, in which Austria and France more or less agreed about their territorial claims in Italy. By the treaty of Utrecht Victor Amadeus II of Savoy acquired the title of King of Sicily, but a few years later, in 1720, he exchanged Sicily for Sardinia and the duchy of Savoy became part of the Kingdom of Sardinia. What the people of the two islands or other Italians thought about this exchange was of little account; they were not asked for their views. Yet 1713 is an important date for Italy. Unity was to be achieved under the descendants of Victor Amadeus II.

In 1796 Napoleon invaded Italy, but it was not until 1804 that he was able to crown himself king of Italy in Milan Cathedral. His influence, or rather that of the French Revolution, remained considerable after his fall, and one may say that it had a decisive effect on the question of Italian unity. It would be inaccurate to say that after his disappearance from the scene the whole of Italy was longing for freedom. The ordinary people, who had difficulty enough in earning their daily bread and only wanted to be left in peace by the Austrian police, were not looking for trouble. It was the intellectuals and the business men who demanded freedom, a constitutional government and independence. They found spokesmen in the Milanese novelist Alessandro

Manzoni, who had been influenced in his youth by the French rationalists and became world-famous through his novel *I Promessi Sposi,* (The Betrothed; 1825), and in the poet Giacomo Leopardi, a fierce patriot. In 1815 the period of the underground movements began, the period of the Charcoal Burners, *I Carbonari,* so called because the leaders originally used to meet in the forests. Italians began to speak of the *Risorgimento,* the resurgence of the Italian spirit, to which the country was indebted for its greatest centuries. In 1831 Giuseppe Mazzini set up a legal organization called Young Italy, with the object of making propaganda for unity. An outstanding member of this organization was Garibaldi, who however, had to flee, because he did not approve of what is now called non-violent resistance. In Italy, too, the year 1848 was a year of rebellion and revolution. Even the Pope gave his subjects a constitution; so did the King of Sardinia and Ferdinand II of Naples and the Two Sicilies. The constitutions were withdrawn again in 1849, as they were elsewhere in Europe; the only one which survived was that of Sardinia, thanks to King Charles Albert, a late convert to more liberal ideas. In 1850 he took Camillo di Cavour into his cabinet. He must have often had difficulties with him, for he had acquired in Cavour an exceptionally capable Minister of Foreign Affairs, who knew exactly what he wanted, the unification of Italy under a liberal government, and who himself was a man of complete integrity, although in politics he had absorbed the lessons of Machiavelli. To forward his aims, he took part in the Crimean War on the side of England and France, although it was difficult to demonstrate that Sardinia had ever had difficulties with Russia. In 1858 he concluded an alliance with Napoleon III of France, who undertook to help in the liberation of Italy from the Alps to the Adriatic - a somewhat vague formula. In exchange for this help France was to get Nice and Savoy. In 1859 Sardinia and France declared war on Austria. After the victory Sardinia acquired Lombardy, and in 1860 Tuscany, Parma and Modena were incorporated. Garibaldi invaded Sicily, and in the same year all the papal states except Rome were conquered. In 1861 Victor Emanuel II of Sardinia became king of Italy. It was not until 1866 that Venice became Italian, after a fresh war with Austria, and it was 1870 before Rome was occupied. Cavour died in 1861. He was the practical thinker who had found a way to convert into reality the ideal of Dante, Machiavelli and the men of the Risorgimento.

In 1866 the history of Northern and Central Italy comes to an end; in other words, it becomes the history of Italy, of a country that had to go through many trials before it plucked the fruits of unity. One may wonder whether this has happened even now. Many people in Lombardy may well have wondered whether they would have been involved in the Fascist period if the north had still been independent. They had the consolation that the partisan movement was very active in the north. It was there that Mussolini was shot dead, and it was no accident that after his death he was exhibited to the public in Milan. Northern Italy had just lived through a period when it was once again separated from the south, in the last months of the Second World War, after Rome and the region to the south of it had been liberated. At Salo, on Lake Garda, Mussolini had set up a new government — history repeated itself this time — under the strict supervision of the Germans. On this occasion the division did not last for centuries. The history of northern Italy is now the history of Italy, although, as we shall see, the long centuries in which it was otherwise have left their traces behind them.

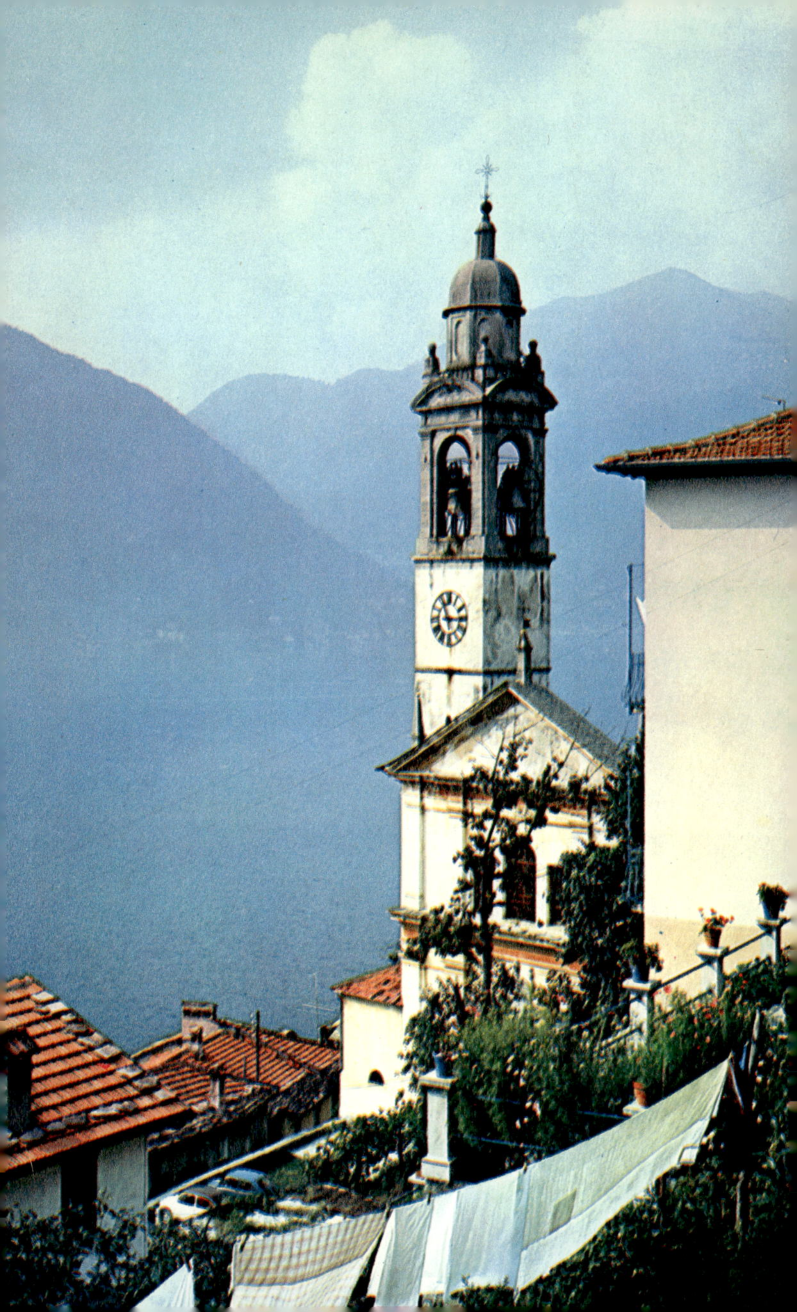

◀ 17. Lake Como: Nesso

18/19. Dolomites

20. Sirmione: Lake Garda

21. Lake Como: Bellagio

22. Fruit galore

23. Malcesine: Lake Garda

24. Isola Bella, Lake Maggiore

25. Lake Garda

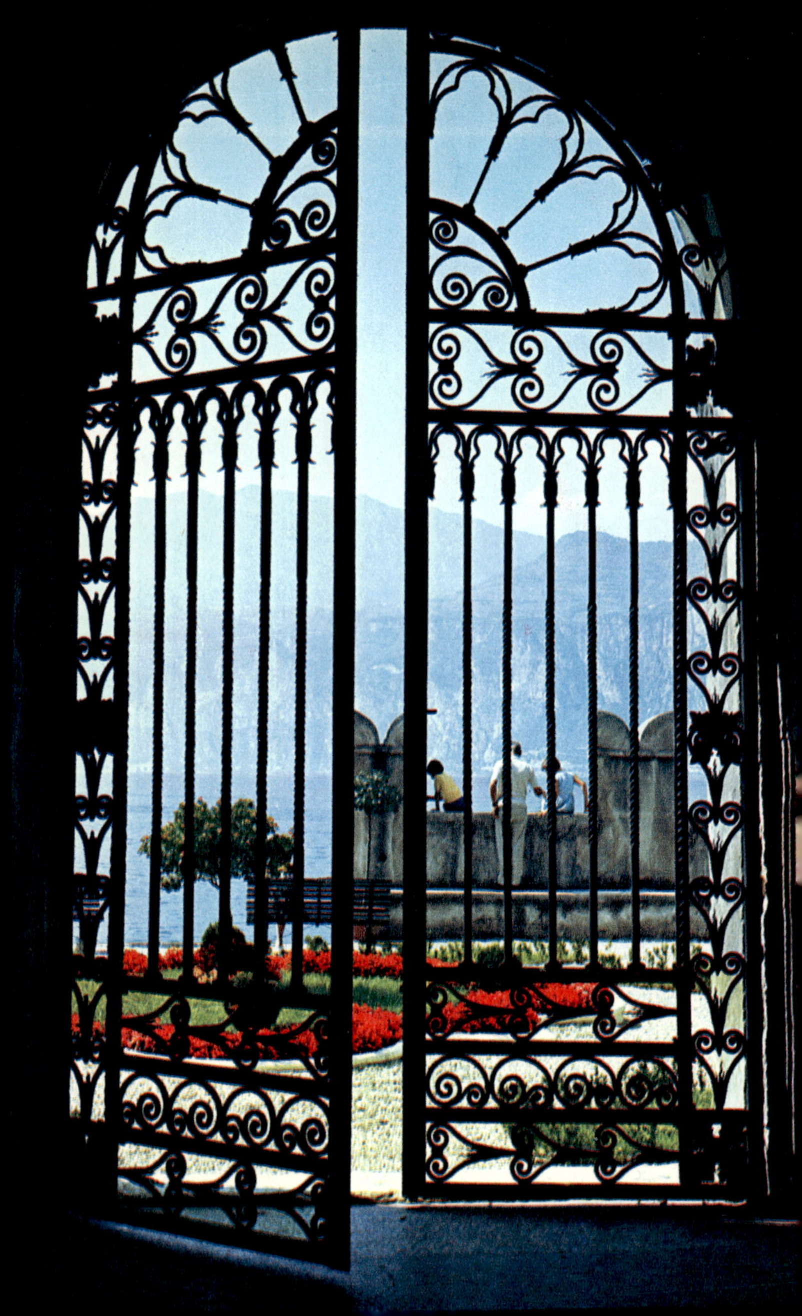

27. Lake Garda, near Riva
◀ 26. Lake Garda, Limone

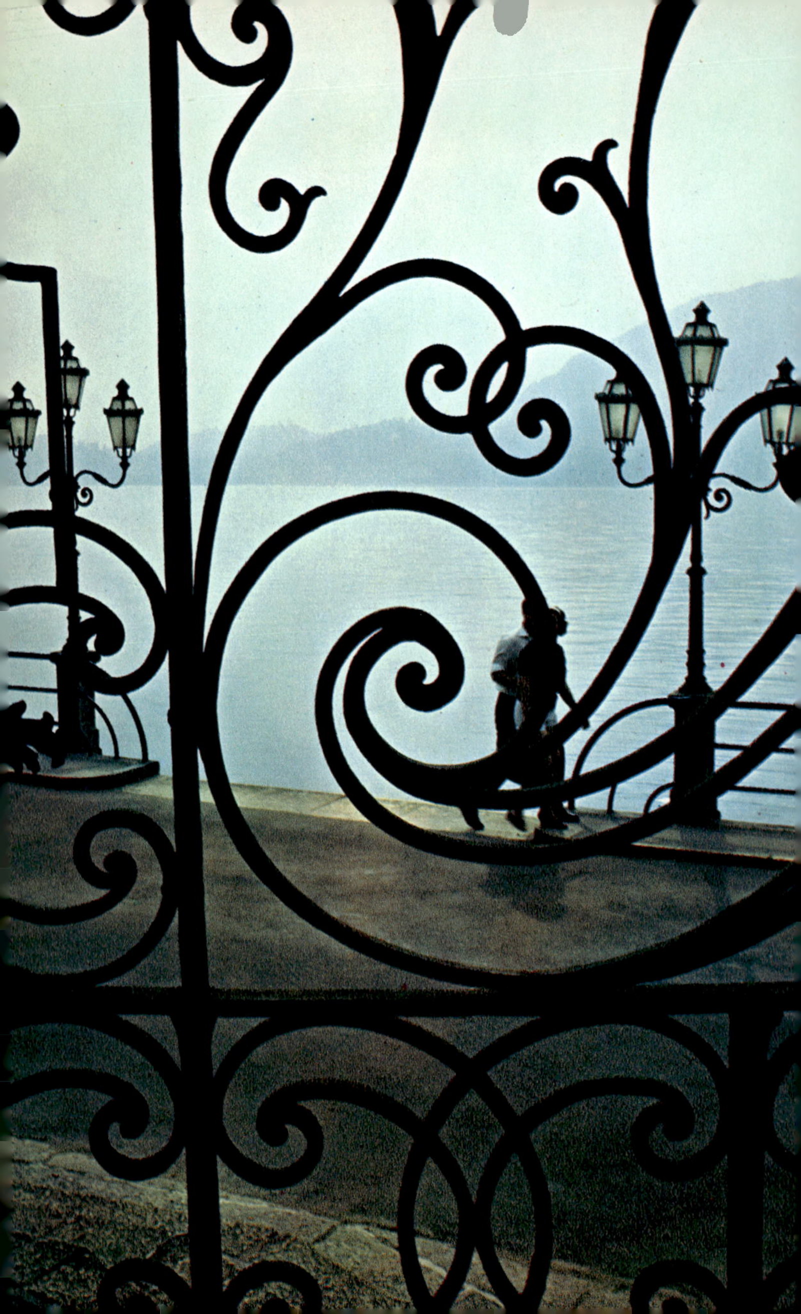

29. Isola Bella, Lake Maggiore
28. Villa Carlotta Tiemezzo, Lake Como
30. Milan
31. Milan Cathedral

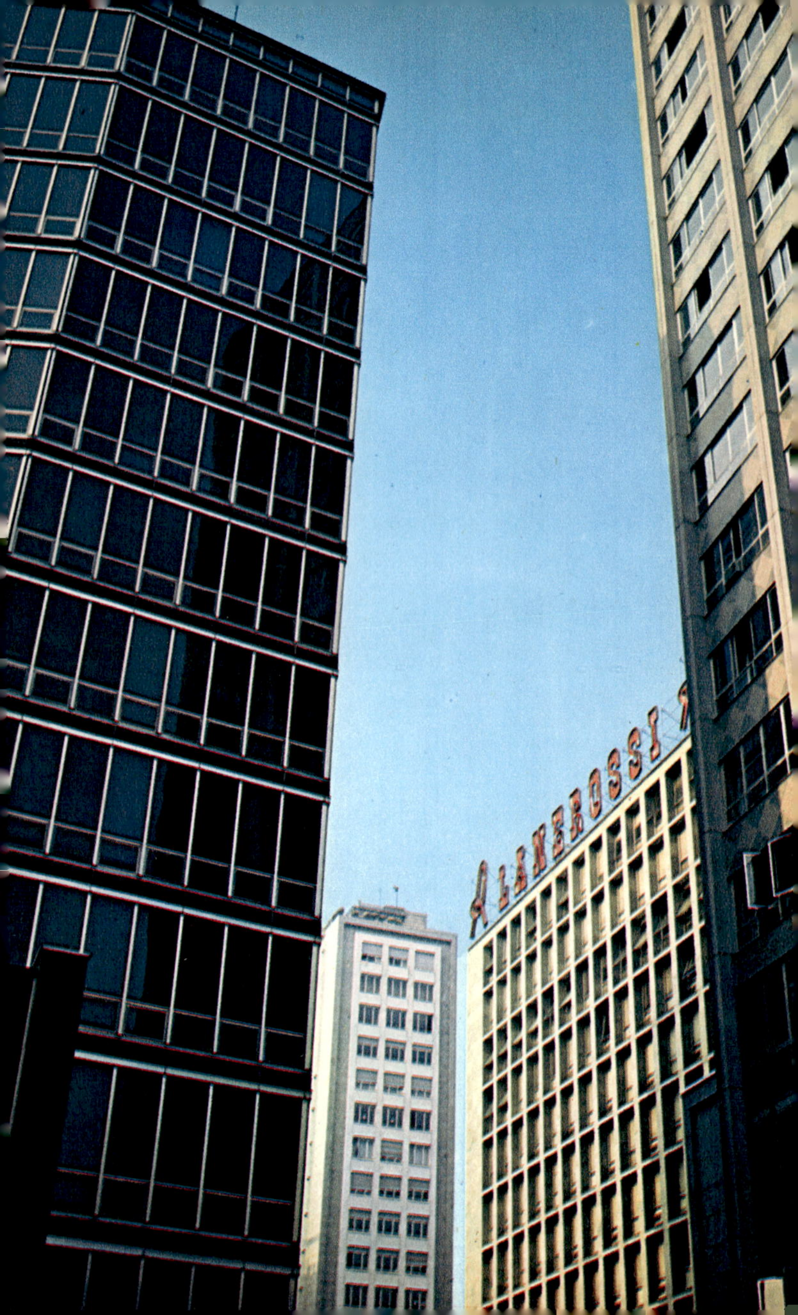
LANEROSSI

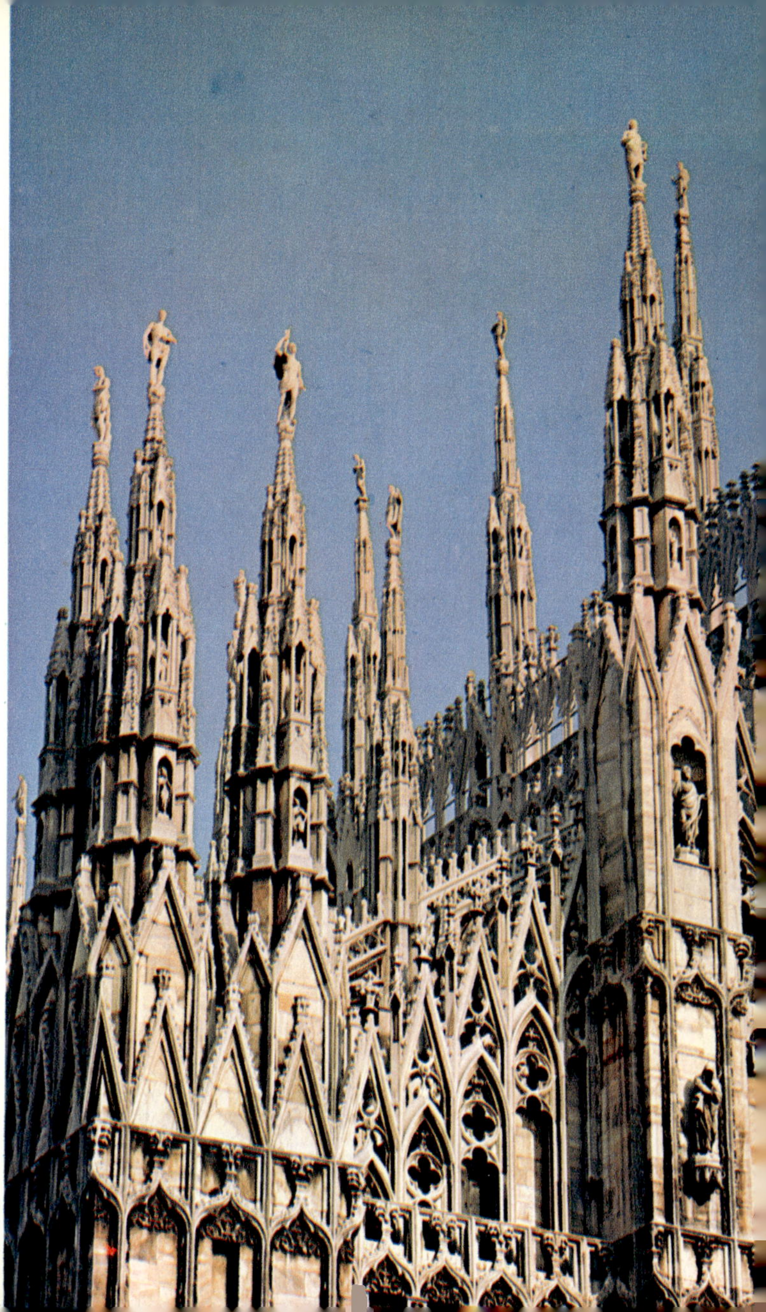

32. Milan, The Gallery

TOWN AND COUNTRY

It is not only their tumultuous, restless history that has left its mark on the Italians. According to many writers, the Italian fits into his landscape. The serious, hard-working farmers of the Po valley are different from the people who grow the Chianti grapes of Romagna or the inhabitants of lovely Umbria, which Raphael and other painters were so fond of using as a background for their saints. We shall deal with the people of northern Italy later; for the moment we want to say something about the land in which they live, about the towns and villages which they have built, although it is difficult to be completely silent about the people whose handiwork is so clearly visible everywhere in the landscape, even — to a certain extent — in the mountains. It is certainly visible all over the lowlands, especially in all the buildings, whether of brick or stone. The unity between the Italian landscape and the towns that have arisen in it has often been praised, and the bonds between town and surrounding country frequently become oppressive.

So far as the big cities of northern Italy are concerned these ties are less intimate. Milan, Turin and Genoa have developed differently, Milan and Turin as industrial cities and Genoa as an international port. They are not typically Italian. I remember how, long ago, I arrived in Milan for the first time, by train. It was a dark, rainy day; from Domodossela on the frontier the mountains had been shrouded in mist. The station was large and murky; the city was cold, and had little of the south about it. "Is this Italy then?" I thought. There were some skyscrapers, which have subsequently made way for other, taller ones. Everything looked very northern, and when I later heard Milan called 'the Manchester of Italy' I was in whole-hearted agreement with the description. Since then I have seen the city from time to time in the hot sun and I have spent many hours sitting outside the cafés of the Galleria, where men walk the whole day through, often arm in arm, as if they had nothing at all to do. Milan is certainly thoroughly Italian. A Frenchman wrote that it longs to be a capital city again. It was the capital of the duchy of Milan and later, under Napoleon, capital of a considerable part of Italy, but never capital of the whole country. That is why people in Milan are bitter about the useless bureaucrats of Rome, who are always thinking up new and superfluous forms, while the poor Milanese have to slave away and pay taxes to support these good-for-nothings.

People say that capital cities are not typical of the country: London is not England, Paris is not France, Amsterdam is not Holland, and according to the Milanese Rome is certainly not Italy. Capital cities seem fated to lose some of the typical features of the countries in which they lie. Milan is an international city, a metropolis, a centre of trade and industry but it is not difficult to find Milanese who have never been outside the city and have never seen Lake

Milan Gallery

Corriere Lombardo
Il P.R.I. esclude il quadri-partito
Luglio ottimo

Como or a farmer's wife in the costume of the Brianza region. No doubt poverty has something to do with this, but not a great deal; it is also partly due to the feeling that outside the city there is nothing worth putting oneself out to see. Roads to the world outside are certainly not lacking. Milan sits like a spider in the middle of a web of roads leading to some glorious areas: to the north are the Alps and the lake district — Lake Maggiore and Lake Como; to the east, Lake Garda. Lombardy, of which Milan is the capital, is a richly blessed region; it has everything — mountains, valleys and the plain of the Po, once an inland sea and now the most fertile part of Italy. Sometimes, amid the canals and poplars, you would think you were in Holland, but the rye and barley are often replaced by rice, and the tulips by mulberry trees with their silk worms.

Autumn in the north

Milan's prosperity is built on the surrounding district, for it is still the biggest silk market in Europe, but it also has all kinds of industries — chemical factories and metal works — which have no connection with the country round about. There is nothing rural about it.

The same is true of Turin. It was once asserted that Turin is Fiat. The big car factory is certainly powerful, and it is run on fairly patriarchal lines, with all the good and bad consequences of this, but it is not true that every family lives under the supervision of the management, even in the sitting-room; and the wages are attractive. People work hard in Turin, and they grumble a good deal at the frivolous Southerners who come up here looking for jobs and are ready to work for less than a fair wage. The local mentality is hard. In the realm of art Piedmont, of which Turin is the capital, has never produced anything of significance. None of the world-famous artists like Michael Angelo or Leonardo da Vinci was born in Turin or ever worked there. It is a somewhat dull city. It did not grow slowly, like most cities in Italy and other countries too. It is certainly old; it was captured in 217 B.C., after a siege lasting three days, by the Carthaginian general Hannibal; but it looks new. It was considerably enlarged in the eighteenth century by the kings of the House of Savoy. The streets are straight and broad. Turin was designed by architects, at one blow. This seldom seems to be a success, as the Australians can bear witness; they built their capital, Canberra, on a lonely plain, because Sydney and Melbourne grudged each other the honour of becoming the capital. Like Canberra, Turin has something artificial about it. Little was left to chance; everything is well thought out and was probably discussed innumerable times by the achitects who drew up the plans. The result is solid and dignified, but devoid of surprises; fantasy is lacking, and that is un-Italian.

The surrounding district is beautiful, but French tourists who know the mountains in the south-east of their own country find that there is little difference here. So, according to them, there is no point in going to Italy. This may be the reason why this corner of Italy is seldom recommended by travel agencies, the region not having sufficient character. Genoa is a different proposition. It makes its living out of the sea. The port looks rather untidy, more so than other ports. As in many other cities, there has been an outburst of building here in the last few years: new skyscrapers are rising up all over the hills. They do not add to the beauty of the city. The most typical parts of it are the narrow streets in the harbour district. They remind one of the lower-class quarters of Naples: the houses are tall, usually something is hanging out to dry and often little sun penetrates, but these streets are full of life. They are always swarming with people. In Naples it is genuine Neapolitans who live in these alleys, but the inhabitants of the *carruggi* of Genoa are a mixture of southern nationalities.

One would say that many of the seamen in Genoa had deserted their ships. On hot days one can understand why, for there are few things more attractive than a cool, dark wine-parlour in this quarter, from which one can watch the bustle. In this city one can also understand why Christopher Columbus, whose birthplace is pointed out with some pride, sailed as far away as possible, accidentally discovering America in the process. In those days Genoa must have been different; now it looks out of place in its surroundings. It is certainly a pity about the landscape.

Some two thousand years ago the poet Vergil sang the beauty of his native town, Mantua, which "nurtured swans as white as snow on its river, with its grassy banks, clear springs and its meadows that will never let the sheep go hungry." It is a poetic picture. The city lies on the rivers Po and Mincio, which flow down from Lake Garda. Mantua

Genoa: Statue of Columbus

was a strong city; it was ruled in the great days by the Gonzagas, a family which knew how to maintain its position in the golden age of the Renaissance without calling on the help of hired murderers. The great court painter was Mantegna. His splendid frescoes adorn some of the rooms of the castle, which is extremely strong — for the Gonzagas were no fools and knew how to defend themselves — but without these works would have certainly looked rather gloomy.

The city has kept something rural about it, in spite of the noise in its busy streets. Perhaps this comes about through its markets, for Mantua is the centre of a flourishing agricultural area. From the ducal palace you look out over a fertile region with polders that have been enclosed in the course of centuries by dykes, and canals that serve only for irrigation. People talk more about the harvest than about Mantegna; in the first half of this century the production of grain was doubled, and there are two and a half times more cows than there were fifty years ago. If you talk about the Gonzagas and the famous past, you will probably be told that they were the best horse-breeders in Europe — which is true — thanks to the excellent grass, and that it is a pity that the interest in horses is declining.

Verona, less than an hour's drive to the west, is where Stradivarius worked. He died there in 1737, and there is still a violin factory, the Scuola Internazionale di Luteria. The inhabitants are proud of him, in a quiet way. He was fond of money — "as rich as Stradivarius" is an expression current in Cremona, his native town. He himself could ask five pounds for a violin; now his instruments are sold for £ 25,000 pounds and more. But all this is the past; what we are now concerned with in the first place is the Po valley. In the province of Cremona there are about 22,000 farms. Most of them are small, some very big. The Sorisinese milk co-operative is the biggest in Europe, and no-

Carabinieri

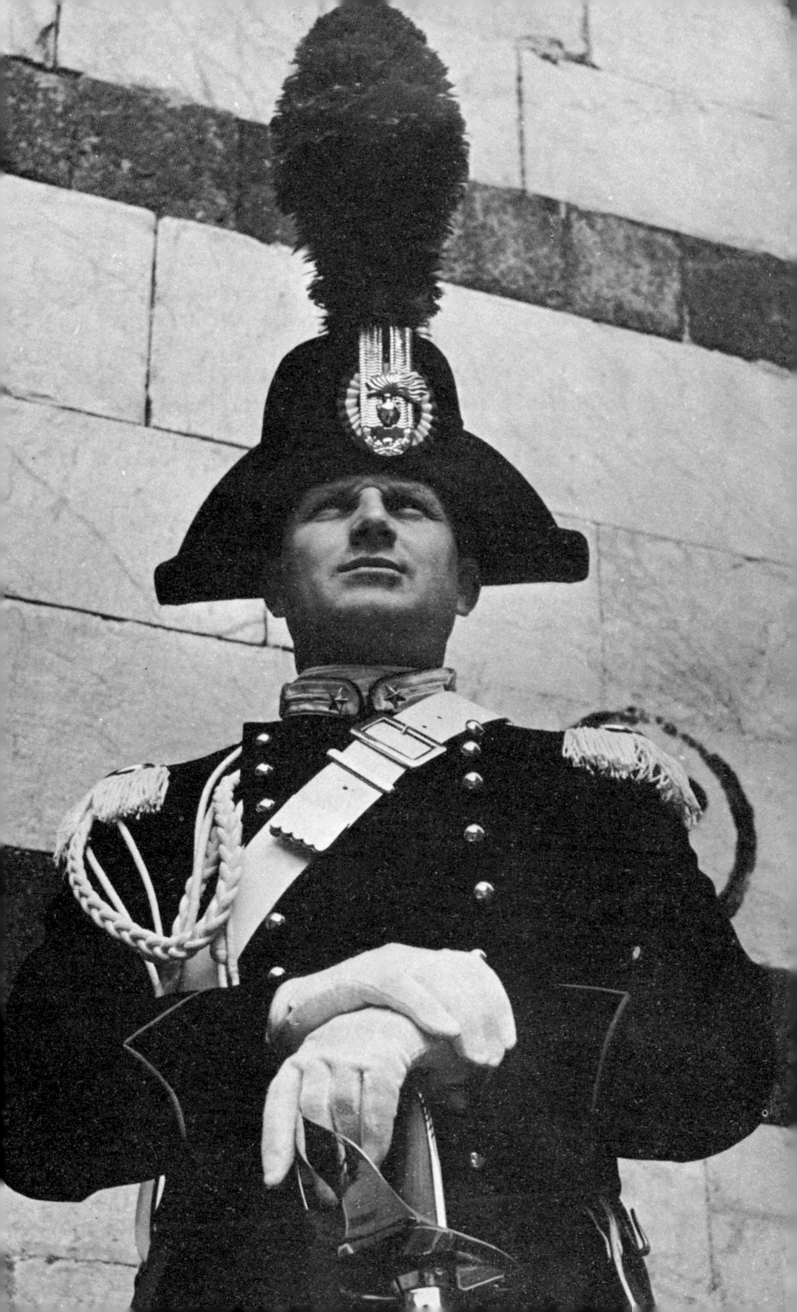

where in Italy are there more pedigree cattle than in this province.

It is a prosperous land to look upon, and in fact it is the richest part of Italy, so they say. Half the population is employed in agriculture. Yet there is still over-population; many thousands of people from this region work in the factories of Milan and Turin, and also abroad. That is one of the reasons why the Po region is left-wing. The prosperity, which in any case is purely relative, has only come about in the years since the war. Before that it was a poor area. There was a strong partisan movement, which won its spurs fighting against the Nazis, after the fall of Mussolini in 1943. The Communists wielded considerable influence in it, and they made use of the opportunity to establish themselves in a powerful position. Many a rich farmer who had done good service in the resistance was liquidated in those days because he was too 'capitalistic' and too hard on his employees. The Po valley is the land of Don Camillo, the good, quick-tempered parish priest and Peppone, the Communist mayor of his village in Guareschi's stories (best-sellers in many countries) who fought together against the Nazis and after the war, are continually at loggerheads. The writer presents the relations between the good Catholics, those who vote for the Christian Democratic party, and the Communists in a somewhat rose-coloured, too friendly light. However, it is true that in the country the Communist leaders adopt a conservative, indeed even capitalistic attitude. The workers on the concerns that are in their hands usually live in the towns, in Cremona, Bologna or Ravenna; they spend an eight-hour working day on the farm and then go home in the evening on their scooters or bicycles. In the south of Italy the farmers live in compact villages on high places, far from their land. There they were able to escape malaria and the armies that used to plague the country in days gone by. It was necessity that drove them to this course.

Now the farm workers — those in the Po valley, that is to say — live from choice in the towns. There they help a good deal to keep the Communists in power, as in Bologna for example. A Communist city, and one of the most beautiful in Europe into the bargain. It is also the city that prides itself most on its cooking. Generally speaking, the Italians are not gourmets like the French. Some of them deny this proposition violently; they say that they are fond of the natural taste of meat and vegetables, and that the Italian cook does not need to hide deficiencies in the way of stale or inferior material under tasty sauces, as his French colleagues do. The best is good enough for the customer of the restaurant in Bologna. That is what they say, and it is true. For many years the mayor, Signor Dozza, has been a living advertisement for his city. He is a Communist, a very moderate Communist, a good one, as even his opponents admit, and ne is fat. He has lived through difficult times, for when Mussolini was in power he had to flee. He thoroughly enjoys Bolognese cooking. He is a typical Italian and, like his fellow-countrymen, suffers from an atavistic hunger. People have suffered from hunger for many generations, and those who can afford to eat enough do so. An Italian restaurant is an eating-house; it is seldom very luxurious, and the somewhat overdone decorations consist of chianti bottles and foodstuffs — big sausages and mountains of fruit. Even in this city of gourmets great dishes of spaghetti are served, though it is true that is more discussion of the quality of the sauce here than in other places. The sauce is in fact outstandingly good, like the spaghetti itself, in which the eggs are not spared.

Guido Piovene, in his book *Journey through Italy*, says that in Bologna he had a meat dish consisting of pheasant, wild duck, another water bird, whose name I do not remember", wild boar, hare and a thrush into the bargain. All these things came from the surrounding countryside. This is always pointed out to the visitor. It is the same in Parma, which also lies in Emilia, the region of which Bologna is the capital. Parma is a city of reddish brick, with many churches, baked for centuries by the hot sun. I have sometimes driven there from Spezia on the Mediterranean, through the cool mountains. Perhaps that is why I find the town so hot. Many people visit Parma because of memories of Stendhal's novel, *La Chartreuse de Parme*. The book is assiduously studied there by literary societies, although Stendhal himself seldom visited the town, and never for longer than a few hours.

Napoleon's wife, Marie-Louise, ruled there when he was languishing on St. Helena. That draws many French people to Parma. The first time I stayed there I was on the way to Canossa, to see the castle where the German emperor Henry IV waited three days with bare feet in the snow for forgiveness from Pope Gregory VII. I wanted to eat Parmesan cheese in Parma for once. A waiter pointed out to me that Parmesan ham was still better. It came from the neighbourhood, he said respectfully, and served it up as if he were performing a sacred rite.

People speak of fat Bologna and frugal Florence, a city of stone. If you drive from Bologna along the motorway to Florence — perhaps the most beautiful stretch of motorway in Europe — you see the difference. Bologna lives on the fat of the land; around Florence grapes and olives grow in abundance, but this mountainous region is relatively infertile and cannot be compared with the Po valley. Yet ancient Florence, with its turbulent history and fierce quarrels, is also a rural city. Not that it has many green parks; the Italian finds the space inside his walled towns too precious for that, and trees have their place in nature. Florence is suited to its surroundings. All round the city one sees the bluish hills, with the silvery olive trees and dark cypresses which adorn the landscape everywhere in Romagna, as they do in Provence, where they made such an indelible impression on Vincent van Gogh. Michael Angelo obtained marble, a quarry of it for himself, when he had to build for the lords of Florence, the Medici. Nothing was too good for their churches and palaces once they were rich, but even then the plain stone from the surrounding mountains was used for the less monumental buildings. The result is a harmonious whole. It will be difficult to preserve this in the long run. It has been said that there is too much art in Florence; for a tourist with two or three weeks' holiday it is impossible to work through it all. There is little of the character of Milan and Genoa, apart from the skyscrapers, though efforts are made to keep the hills round Florence as free as possible from this evil. There is hardly a place in the neighbourhood that is not famous for one reason or another — because it is depicted by a well known painter or mentioned in a poem, or because a great man worked there. The gentlemen of the commission for historical monuments have a hard task, for Florence is not just thrifty; it is positively stingy. Experts say that even the landscape in Tuscany is calculating.

Umbria is all softness, but even in the land of chianti "one discovers underneath the graceful surface precision and a

Milan: The Gallery

cold strictness of design". The soil is poor; round Siena and along the old road to Rome the thin layer of earth has disappeared from the hills and the chalk has come to the surface. Piedmont and all the mountainous regions, both in the Dolomites and the Apennines, are green, even after a hot summer. In Tuscany however one can imagine the farmers looking out anxiously for a shower of rain, even though vine and olive thrive in the heat.

The wine of this district, chianti, is the Italian wine best known abroad, where many wines take precedence over chianti. There are some famous brands, but relatively little has been done to 'push' the best wines. In this respect the French are far ahead of the Italians, although many Italian wines could perfectly well compete with those of France.

From an Etruscan tombstone, Tarquinia

Everywhere on the Côte d'Or efforts are made to entice the foreigner into the wine-cellars; in Poggibonsi, the centre of the chianti trade, scarcely any interest in him is shown, although this seems to be changing slowly now.

In any case, Tuscany is richer than Umbria. The traveller could easily forget this because of the landscape, which is always glorious, both in the flat region near Assisi and in the mountains. The poverty so obvious in the villages between Rome and Naples and further south is less evident here. The farmsteads are small, and the higher they lie the more picturesque they look. However, many of them have no proper drinking water; the stony ground demands hard work and gives only a small return. There are too few roads and too little irrigation. It is all a bit medieval, like Perugia, the biggest town. In Perugia there are Etruscan walls, a museum with many medieval paintings and few buildings erected later than the sixteenth century; there are tradesmen who use the same methods as their forefathers in the fourteenth century. Like so many other towns, including Assisi, Perugia lies on a hill-top. Its citizens can — and frequently do — enjoy the view over the surrounding countryside. It is a region with proud memories, especially of St. Francis, but one whose inhabitants walk through life bowed under the problems caused by too long a period of neglect, in spite of the thriving tourist industry. In Perugia you hear foreign languages spoken as often as Italian, and there are special parking places for foreign cars. You also frequently hear the complaint that one cannot live on beauty alone.

Italy is often called a living museum. There is something of this about Umbria. "The ancient gods have not left this place, which was once dedicated to them... Here the present is one with the past." It does not completely tally. In days gone by, the creatures in one of the rivers turned white by the grace of the gods. All that is past, and St Francis is no longer there to give new life to vineyards, as he once did in Rieti. The old stories are still told, the old art collections are admired, the churches are well maintained, but the beauty is deceptive. Even in the prettiest places of northern and central Italy people would be glad to have rather more of the pleasures of modern life. This is certainly the case in Venice, the city that has become one big museum. Not that its inhabitants have anything against this; they are very conscious of living in the most beautiful city in the world, even though it seems to be slowly — very slowly — sinking away. People accept the inconveniences involved as part of the bargain. They walk endless distances because a gondola is expensive and there are more bridges than gondolas; moreover, every Venetian knows that you can see the city better on foot than from a boat. People live on top of each other in decaying houses, dozens of which have been declared uninhabitable, but for which they pay a monthly rent of about one and sixpence, to the despair of the owners, who cannot keep them in decent repair. Venice is perhaps the most painful case in Italy, the south not excluded. This is quietly accepted, or perhaps it is not; in any case it is clear from more than one investigation that the most wretchedly housed citizens do not want any other house, or at any rate not one outside Venice. In this respect it is the strongest city in Italy, although the characteristics of the Venetians are also reflected elsewhere. This is the strength of the Italian people.

33. The island of San Giorgio Maggiore, Venice

34. Gondola (detail), Venice

35. Piazza San Marco, Venice

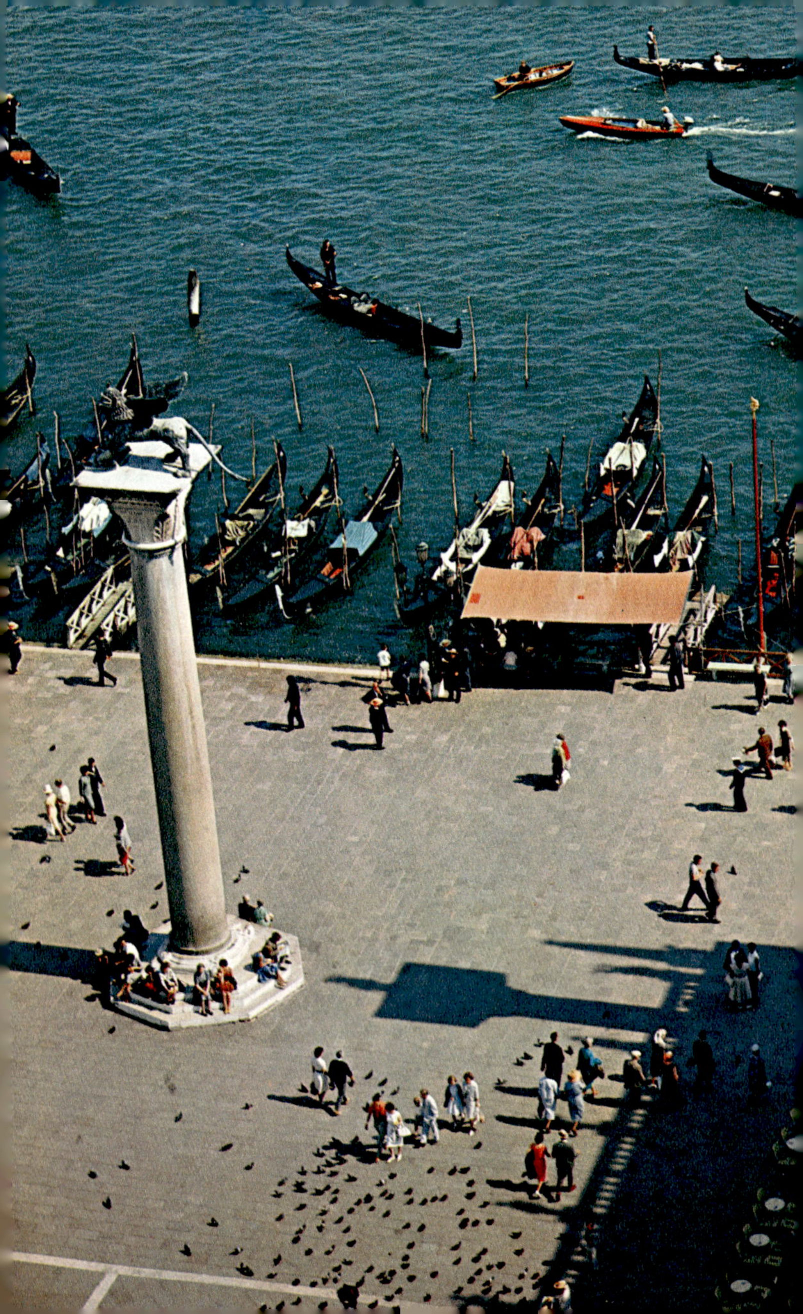

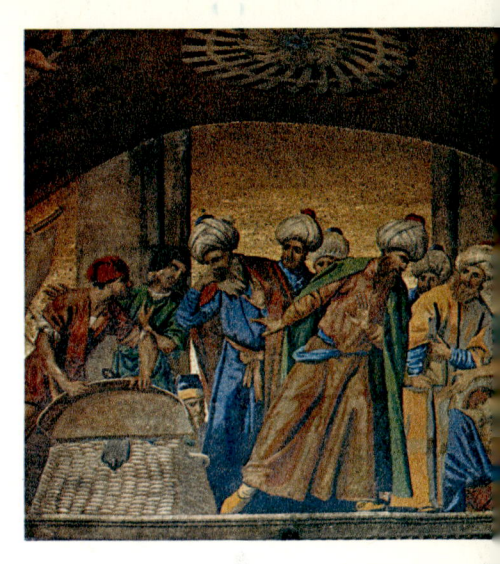

37. Mosaic in San Marco
36. Piazetta San Marco and Grand Canal

38. Murano glassware, Venice
39. Venice: one of the many smaller canals ▶

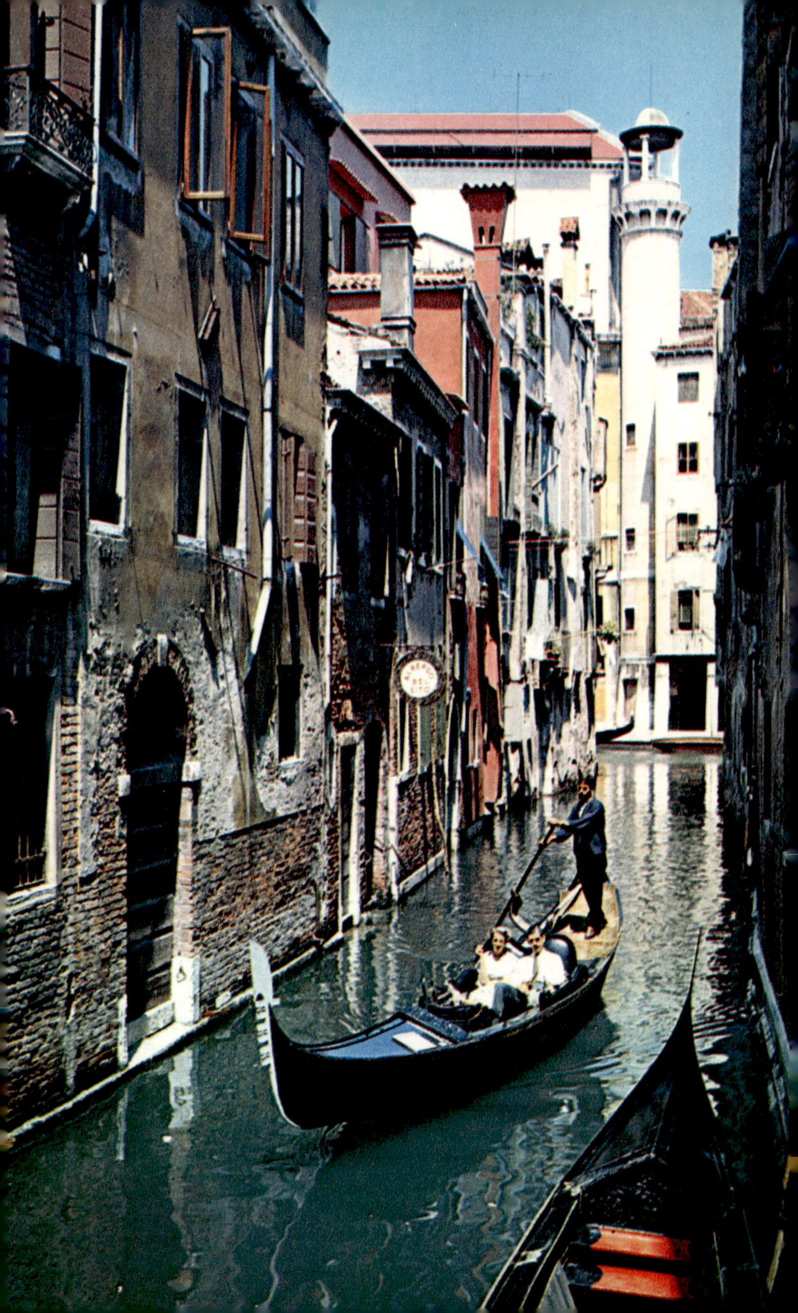

MAXIMIANVS

41. Galla Placidia, Mausoleum, Ravenna (mosaic)
40. Ravenna, San Vitale: Mosaic of the Empress Theodora

42. Orvieto: a Tuscan cattle market

43. San Gimignano

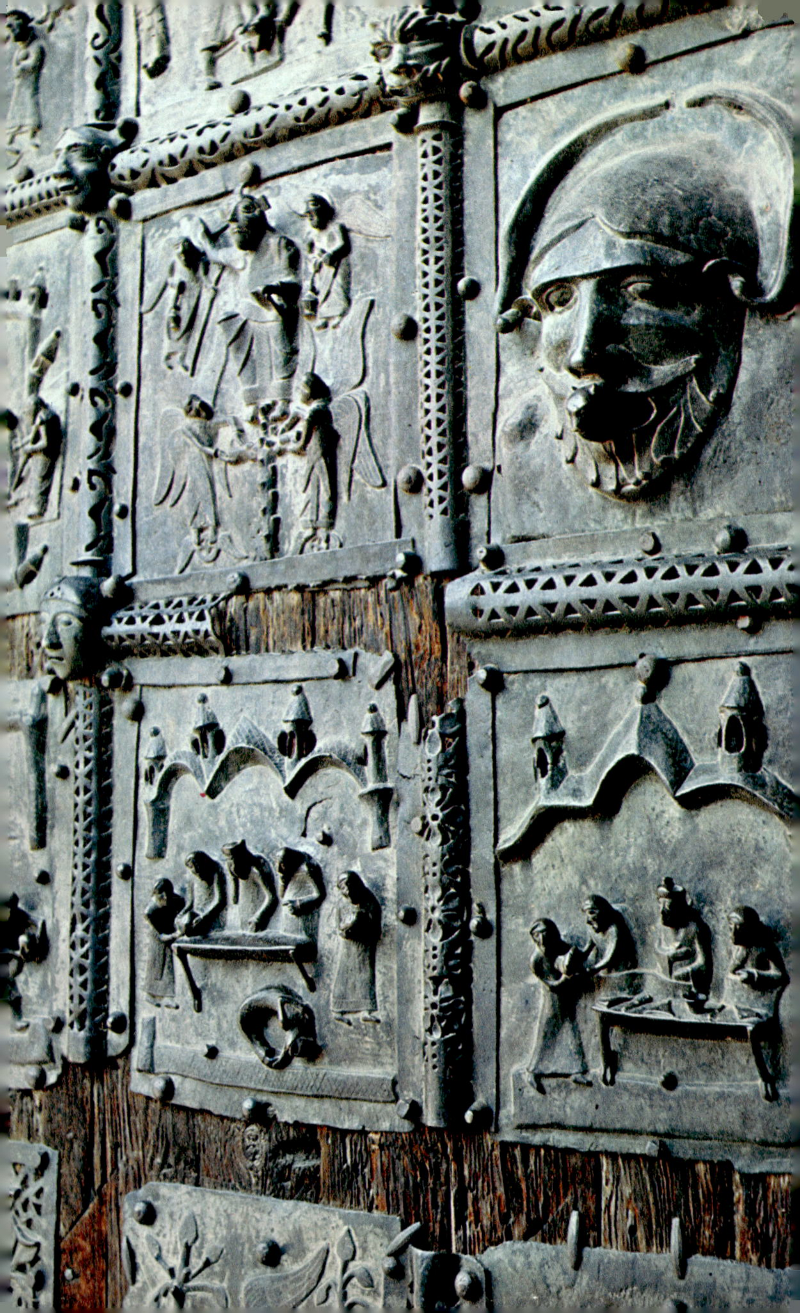

45. Verona: Ponte Scaligero
44. Verona: San Zeno Maggiore church door

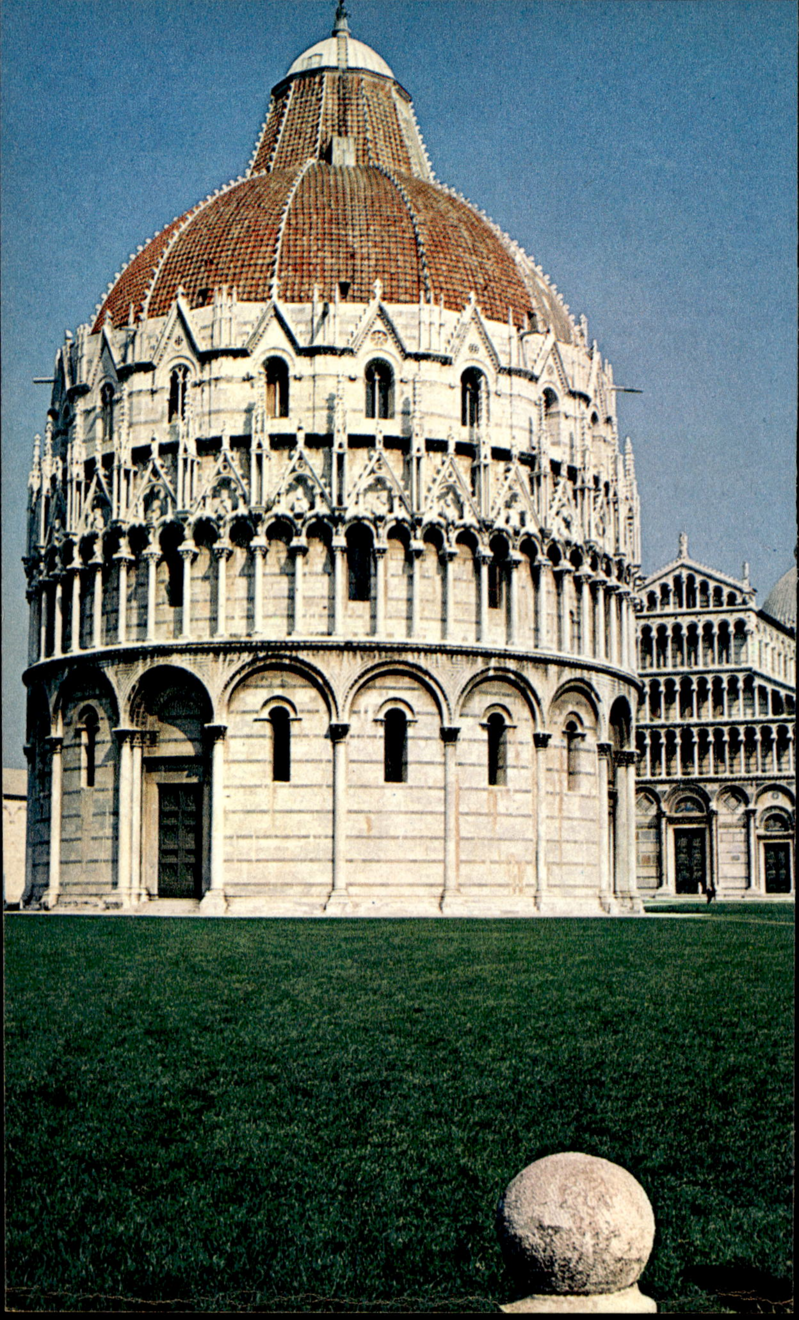

47. Pisa: Cathedral
◀ 46. Pisa: Baptistry, Cathedral and Leaning Tower

48. Assisi, San Francesco Basilica

THE PEOPLE

"The Italian is lazy, He is a thief. He talks too much. He is a coward. He is illiterate." This list could easily be extended from books by foreigners who, after a visit to Italy, have put down their impressions on paper. Many a northern Italian would agree enthusiastically with these reproaches, but he would point out that they refered to the southern Italians. Some northerners might even go a shade further. A Milanese would not hesitate to make a violent attack on the people of Turin. Anyone born in Venice will have a poor opinion of the Veronese, although he may admit that there are a lot of pretty girls there, a fact which every visitor can note for himself. In Florence it is difficult to elicit a good word about the inhabitants of Pisa or Lucca. The only thing that northerners are agreed upon is that few southern Italians are worth much. This conviction is universal. A second certainty is that one's town or region is far superior to any other part of Italy. Every country has its own local chauvinism. The Scot finds it a little difficult to have affection for the Englishman or to estimate him at his true worth.

Many people from the northern part of Holland are only too ready to talk about the backwardness of the Limburgers, while the latter know that their province is the most beautiful in the country. In Italy these primitive feelings of one's own excellence and the inferiority of one's neighbours seem to be stronger than elsewhere. A French writer wonders if Italy really is a unity; certainly in France mutual criticism is not nearly so fierce. However, in practice it tends to exceed expectations. No one is more convinced of the perfection of his city and his way of life than the Venetian. He will say, "We do that in such-and-such a way", and by that he means that any other mode of behaviour is not only ridiculous but even criminal. Once I met a Venetian painter called Morosini. He proudly informed us that he was a descendant of the doge of this name, "a real pirate". Later I discovered that the whole staff of the doges were permitted to take the family name of their master, so that very probably my friend was justified in priding himself on his connection with the noble house of Morosini. What he was still prouder of was the piracy of these forefathers and his Venetian descent. He was penniless, but thoroughly enjoyed our wine, "wine from the neighbourhood of Venice", as he asserted with an air that seemed to imply that he would have accepted nothing else. That we had visited other places in Italy besides his own city was incomprehensible to him and a sign that there were deficiencies in our good taste. We asked if it would not be better for Venice to become independent again, as it was once. No, he said, that was not the aim. It was naturally unjust that Venice was not the capital, but he did not know a single Venetian who advocated secession. Then the Tyroleans caught it — the lunatics in South Tyrol who were agitating for incorporation in that completely ludicrous country, Austria. We were also informed that the renewal of the Church had started in Venice. Was not good Pope John XXIII a Venetian? We said that he had certainly been Patriarch of Venice but had been born, we thought, in the neighbourhood of Bergamo. "A north Italian in any case!" retorted Morosini, adding that he had never let anyone forget this. Did I not know, he asked, that John liked nothing better than to go and work on the land for a few days with his brothers? His predecessor would have never done that! I pointed out that Pope Pius XII did not come from farming stock. "No, he was a Roman," said Morosini, with a gesture implying the deepest contempt for the capital of his country. His opinions were typical. For the north Italian, one's birthplace is one's most important possession. In earlier times it was often independent and had to be defended by force of arms against rapacious neighbours. That is an indelible memory. Fortunately the old feuds can now be fought out on the football field, and this may be one of the reasons why this sport is so popular. At any rate, the contestants now stay alive. Once when a Milanese friend had poured his heart out to me about the Genoese — "worthless people!" — I ventured to point out that all the same Christopher Columbus did come from Genoa. "That is highly dubious," replied Carlo. But like a good Milanese he really had a still greater dislike for the citizens of Turin.

One cannot accuse the citizens of Turin of laziness or illiteracy. My friend — a *dottore* — was himself too intelligent for that. No, in Turin people work hard; the great objection to the city is that it lacks imagination. Its inhabitants do not know how to enjoy life; they just keep on working and working. In Milan things are different. The people there combine business with pleasure, and there is also some respect for non-material things, such as the opera. The Scala is full for every performance, and of course the Scala at Milan is the most famous opera house in the world, with the best performances. That must be admitted. But I knew that almost everyone obtains free tickets, and that there would perhaps be smaller audiences if the public really had to pay the high official prices.

The greatest failing of the Milanese is their financial optimism. Things have gone well with them; since the Second World War they have made tremendous progress. This cannot go on for ever according to Carlo, and he should know, for he was busy writing a big book on the economic history of Italy, a project that was being financed by a factory. There were no obligations on his side; he was completely free. Everyone, he said, lived on credit. The manufacturers lent money, and people bought everything on hire purchase; it was his belief that there was not a television set or a scooter in the city that was completely paid for. There was really no money with which to pay for the skyscrapers. And then there were the costly motorways. They are indeed costly to drive along; the toll amounts to about twopence a mile. However, that was not Carlo's complaint. He took the view that, if the money had to be thrown away somehow or other, it should have been used to build hospitals. As things are, it is spent on fast roads for foreign tourists. Most Italians cannot afford to pay the toll! One hears so frequently the story of the frivolous way in which money is spent in northern Italy that in the end one has to believe it. The other side of the medal is the story of the hundreds of people who began with nothing after 1945 — making sweets, for example, and selling them in the villages then starting a factory with a few shillings and becoming as rich as Croesus. Ferrero is a good illustration of this. "A real north Italian," said Carlo; "they work hard, too hard, and then usually die from a heart attack, like Ferrero."

The north Italian is not lazy, anymore than the south Italian, if he gets a chance to work. The loafers, who are seldom to be seen in the north these days, usually have no job. What strikes you in all the towns is how late people go on working, especially the small independent tradesmen. They certainly like talking and do a good deal of it. And the Italian is fond of noise. It is not a country in which people go to bed early, and the foreigner will serve his own interests if he remembers this. In many a town I have lain awake until late in the night! Once in Parma it was a smith, who did not know when to stop and went on banging away at his metals with a hammer until long after midnight. Later on he received a visit from his neighbours, and one of those conversations developed which make you think that they are going to degenerate any moment into a thundering row. The participants speak with great emphasis and the atmoshere grows more and more violent, but nothing happens; it is usually a conversation between friends who feel strongly about the subject under discussion. At the same time mother is at loggerheads with the children, or so it seems to the outsider. He cannot understand, particularly if he comes from northern Europe, why they still have to be in the streets so very late at night. One gradually learns that mama's violent reproaches are not reproaches at all; it is simply her normal way of talking. When they are small the children are shamefully spoiled, but they are sent out to work early whenever the family needs the few poor lire that they can earn — which is less and less the case in the north of Italy.

It is true that many Italians are still illiterate, especially the older ones, and in the south the children, too. The reason for this is that their elders cannot bring themselves to send the children to school, as Guareschi makes clear in one of his stories about Don Camillo and Peppone. But discipline and sense of responsibility are often lacking in the education of the little darlings — as I have too often noted to the ruin of my night's rest!

The people themselves in northern Italy hardly seem to notice the noise; on the contrary, the more racket there is, the happier they are. If it is not children, then it is the scooters that made the visitor's life a burden. These vehicles, known as Vespas (wasps), were still relatively few and far between in the first few years after the War. They have won the hearts of the young people, naturally more in the wealthy north than in the poorer south, where the hire-purchase system has necessarily remained within reasonable bounds, as Carlo would put it. It is said that the scooter is a status symbol and for the young man at the same time a means of proving his manhood. However that may be, solid use, or rather mis-use, is made of it. The young men join together in scooter gangs, which roar through the streets until late at night. I believe that these spluttering motors are one of the great differences between pre-war and post-war Italy, and the evil is far and away worst in northern Italy. You find it everywhere, even in Bologna, where the hire-purchase system has had no success because the Bolognese consider it beneath their dignity to live on credit.

Once, after some exhausting weeks, we arrived in Venice, that blessed city without cars or motors. We would finally be able to sleep in peace. But no, it is incredible how hard and busily a few gondoliers can talk after their day's work is finished! The more prosperous young men exchange their scooters for cars as soon as they can. The Italian car industry has made an excellent job of adapting itself to the needs of its customers. Petrol is expensive and although the foreign tourist gets a rebate the cars need to be small. And they are, too, but they are treated mercilessly by the Italians. The greatest misfortune that a car-owner can suffer is to be overtaken, even if he is driving the tiniest baby car and his opponent has several hundred horse-power at his disposal. On the motorways this is not so bad; one just lets the noise and violence pass. But on the old roads, especially in the mountains, it is a different matter. There the speed maniacs tear round the bends, boldby trusting to their horns and the sanity of the people driving in the opposite direction. Really one cannot even accuse them of recklessness, for before starting they have indubitably commended their lives to the Madonna, and who can help them if she can't?

Carlo does not accept this. It was once asserted that there is not a single genuine unbeliever in Italy. The Communists may not go to church every Sunday, so it was said, but they turn up there at the important moments in their lives. So far as southern Italy is concerned, this is certainly true, I think. So far as northern Italy is concerned, it does not quite tally. Carlo gave up his membership of the Communist party in 1957, after the Hungarian rising, but his affection for the Church did not increase as a result. Perhaps he inherited his aversion for it from his father, who was a general in the cavalry when Mussolini came into power.

Siena: Piazza del Campo

He handed in his resignation immediately, not because he had any insuperable objections to Fascism, but because the Fascists were so vulgar. Later, in 1929, when the agreement between Pope Pius XI and Mussolini was signed — the solution to the question of Rome — the father vowed that he would never set foot in a church again. His son became a partisan in 1943, after Musolini had been deposed and there was an official German occupation. He laughs when you begin to talk about piety of the north Italian Communists, who are supposed to be so loyal to their faith. There may well be such people, he says, but he doesn't know any of them. There aren't any among his friends.

Carlo does not look like an Italian; he has blue eyes, like his blonde wife. It irrates him if you talk about this. In the south the people are black-eyed, black-haired and very quick of movement — the Italian type as it is imagined abroad. Everywhere in Milan, along the glorious Ligurian coast from Ventimiglia to Genoa and further on as far as Spezia, one sees people like Carlo. They are descendants of the earlier inhabitants who were there before Rome was founded by Romulus and Remus. And there must certainly be some with the blood of the foreign occupiers in their veins, the blood of the Austrians, the Germans and also the Germanic tribes — Lombards and Goths — who brought the Roman empire to its knees.

"Nor are we womanizers or thieves!" This is a remark that was once made in Carlo's house in Milan, probably by Carlo himself, but perhaps by one of his friends who happened to be there. It was an answer to stories I had told which were based on real experiences, either my own or those of people dear to me. In 1947 I had been the guest of the Dutch consul in Genoa. Every time we stepped out of his car he took a few parts out and locked the steering wheel with a heavy chain. This was necessary, he said, because otherwise his car might be stolen. At that time northern Italy was as poor as the south is now, perhaps even poorer. In the newspapers one read articles about gangs which roamed the countryside. In the hotels, on his advice, I carefully handed in my money at night and in the morning it was politely handed back to me. I used to examine the contents of my cases; nothing was ever missing. In Milan I met, also in 1947, the photographer, Sem Presser, who actually had been robbed of all his possessions in Sicily. But nothing ever happened to me, even when bitter poverty prevailed in the north, not to mention the south. Yet I must emphasize that I have never been robbed of anything in the south either. In the last few years I have certainly been thoroughly swindled on each visit, but a resounding scene, with a bit of screaming — in any language you like — of the same intensity as the locals use, soon puts things right. What is taken amiss is that you don't protest or, if you do protest, that you don't do it at the top of your voice.

We will speak about northern Italy in a moment; first let us deal with the observation that the north Italians are not woman-chasers. The great question is now where the north stops and the south begins; and naturally there are a good many southerners in the north. In any case, in the well-known resorts like Portofino on the Gulf of Genoa or Lido di Jesolo about twenty miles north-east of Venice, it is not advisable for ladies to go down to the beach after dark. In the tourist season the beaches are crowded during the daytime, far too crowded, but the crowd stops as soon as you are a few yards — fifteen at the most — out in the sea. The pretty north Italian girls who visit Lido di Jesolo, girls from Vicenza, Milan and Verona, walk about in luxurious bathing costumes, but they always walk along the edge of the water; they don't do any swimming. In the evening the darlings are in their hotels or bungalows, but there are gentlemen who address, as we must put it, foreign ladies who are taking a walk along the shore. They are all south Italians, according to Carlo. That may well be so, but these things happen in northern Italy as well.

Where does the north stop? Where serious poverty starts, people say nowadays, that is where the south starts, and each year it lies a little further to the south. This is not completely true. Castelammare, a few miles to the south of Naples, is quite a prosperous little town, but there are still villages and small towns to the north where people throw stones at foreign cars. This is usually a sign of poverty, the vindictiveness of little boys against the rich stranger — and to them every tourist they see going by in his expensive car is rich!

In northern Italy now travellers seldom have their cars stolen or damaged. One can quite confidently leave them standing in the street, even if one is staying in a cheap hotel. This is fortunate, for there is little room in the garages, which are expensive anyway.

Once it was more or less customary to say that there was no middle-class, no bourgeoisie in Italy. There were only a great many poor people and a few rich people, but the latter were very rich indeed. This is still the case in the south, but in the north a middle class has come into being. In the south the proletariat leads a wretched existence, and so do many intellectuals, who in spite of their fine-sounding qualifications cannot obtain jobs. In a place like Turin the workers live like middle-class people in beautifully furnished houses. In dress, too, the younger men are indistinguishable from the sons of rich men. Later in life, when he has been married for some years, the Italian prefers a comfortable suit to an elegant one, and also worries less about his figure.

At the casino in Monte Carlo the best customers are Italians, northern Italians, who have made a great deal of money in recent years. They spend their whole holiday there and for the rest of the year sit working hard in their offices. They sometimes grumble at the high wages their workers demand or at the taxes they have to pay, but they respect the work which their men do. It was different in days gone by and still is here and there in the south. In those days one would often hear the term of abuse *contadino* (peasant, or rather 'wretch'). This was the man who worked for a low wage when he could get work at all. In the north he has disappeared. The worker there knows how to stand up for his rights and his employer respects him for it. Respect for human dignity has grown; in earlier days it left much to be desired. This is a post-war development; it is further advanced in northern Italy, but with better social economic conditions it will spread over the whole country.

THE TRAVELLER

The proverb says, as you know, that all roads lead to Rome, but I rather doubt whether you will arrive there on this first trip. That is because there is so much to see on the way; the country is beautiful wherever you cross the frontier — over the Brenner Pass if you travel via South Germany and Austria, over the St. Gothard if you want to see something of Switzerland on the way, or at Ventimiglia if you want to drive along the French and Italian Riviera. You ought to spend two or three weeks there. The guide books will reduce you to despair. It is a good idea to study these useful books before the start of your trip; I have always learnt something even from the worst of them, and the better ones are indispensable, because they draw the reader's attention to innumerable things that he would otherwise miss. The little time you have is too valuable to be wasted by travelling at random. However, the guide books always assume that you have months at your disposal. According to them, you should spend two or three weeks in Venice.

There is much to be said for this, and also for the month that must be earmarked for Florence. In earlier times young men used to go on a grand tour; in the seventeenth century, and even later, they would spend a whole year in Italy. Stendhal exclaimed that "if one has a heart and a shirt, one must sell the shirt in order to live *in questo pezzo di cielo caduto in terra* (in this piece of heaven that has fallen on earth)". Italy has always been cheap — although in the last few years this too has been changed by mass tourism — but one could not hold out very long on the proceeds of a shirt, and the gentlemen who made the grand tours were extremely privileged from the financial point of view. Like most tourists these days, you have had to save up for some time before your trip, but like many young people — and some older people, too — you want to see everything. You want to stroll through old towns and visit museums, you are fond of a beautiful landscape, and you would like to spend at least a few days lazing on the beach. I fear that you will never reach Rome on this first trip.

That is no bad thing. After the young Mozart had been to Italy for the first time, he wrote to his father: "I beseech you, see that I return to Italy, and that I can live there for a little while." He was not the first, or the last, to think like this about Italy. The average modern tourist cannot stay there long, but he can return the following year, and a great many people do this. Rome can wait. On my first visit I did not get any further than the north. I spent my time in cities like Milan, Genoa and Turin, which will surprise you after the earlier pages in this little book. I simply had to limit myself; the only transport at my disposal consisted of the bus and the train and I was interested primarily in art and people. Even now museums can be oases in the bustle, although it is usually advisable to be there when they open and to remember that many are shut on Sunday afternoons. At those times the Italian concentrates his interest mainly on the football matches, as is clear from the noises proceeding from the transistor radios that many take with them on their Sunday excursions, and from the earnestness with which pools forms are studied later in the day, when the results are known. Then innumerable Italians lose one more illusion and just a few become much richer; however, in a week's time there will be another chance to win a few million lire! But back to the museums: the two big ones in Florence, the Galleria degli Uffizi and the Galleria Pitti, the palace in which Marie di Medici lived before she became queen of France, are always crowded. They figure on the programmes of many travel agencies and a visit to the city is incomplete if one has not seen the Botticelli room and the Flemish primitives, just to quote two examples.

Such a visit is an essential part of a trip to Italy. In Milan the crowds are not so bad. In the Brera Museum — entrance free on Sundays — one can even see Rembrandts, pictures by El Greco and Van Dyke, and Mantegna's most famous work, the *Dead Christ*. Mantegna is one of those painters of whom one sees relatively little outside Italy — more's the pity. This makes a trip to Italy worth the trouble. So does the *Last Supper* by Leonardo, in the convent next door to Santa Maria delle Grazie in Milan. Reproductions of it are to be seen all over the world, and there are many stories centering round this fresco, in which Christ and the apostles are depicted at the moment when Jesus is saying that one of his disciples will betray him. It suffered a good deal of damage in the war years. They say that it will gradually disappear completely and that in a few decades nothing will remain of the masterpiece of the man who was not only one of the greatest painters of his time but also, as a French writer has put it, "invented most of our modern civilization; "he foresaw the tank, designed the first aeroplane that flew, and also designed a machine-gun and a submarine." His sketches and also reproductions of 1750 of his prophetic drawings are exhibited in the Biblioteca Ambrosiana, one of the monuments of Milan, named after the great fourth-century bishop, Ambrose, who baptized St. Augustine.

I have tried to explain why I stayed so long in Milan on my first trip to Italy. In summary let me say it was simply because there are incomparably beautiful things there, things which one can see nowhere else and which — some of them, at any rate — are doomed to destruction.

There are still other sights to see in the neighbourhood; more about them in a moment. One does not often discover unknown things on a first trip, however good one's preparations may have been. The most beautiful places are well known, especially in a country that has been in the limelight for so many centuries. The travel agencies know this. They are right to send the tourist to Pisa, for example, for the Leaning Tower is splendid, in spite of a popularity that makes it seem faintly ridiculous to some people, who want to walk untrodden paths. I could spend days in the cathedral square at Pisa. One can always discover something fresh in the Baptistery, built between 1153 and 1278, or in the cathedral (1068-1118), even if it is only that big pieces of the marble used for these buildings came from still earlier Roman buildings; they still bear the old Latin inscriptions! Scholars know this perfectly well, of course, but it is pleasant to make the discovery for oneself. But, once again, you do not discover much as a tourist, and I have often wondered whether it is not better to go the first time with an organized party. The *bona fide* agencies are glad to arrange these for whatever country you wish to visit — though they do not always display a very good grasp of the tourist's powers of endurance. One then obtains an overall view of the country. But like many young people you probably want to see things for yourself — and I speak from my own experience. Anyway, you know now that you must go to Pisa, and you must not omit to visit the 'cemetery' (Campo Santo) and the Museo Nazionale, which is housed in the former monastery of San Matteo. The Campo Santo, behind the Leaning Tower, dates from the twelfth century and was bombed on the 27th July, 1944. According to some guide books it is not worth the trouble of a visit. This merely shows once again that some authors of guide books do not bother to check their facts. The special and enthralling attraction of this cemetery is that the northern Italians are so skilful at restoring their works of art, not only when they have been damaged by a bomb but also when they have been the victims of centuries of neglect. The restorers turn their work into a lesson; they show what a fresco looked like in the past, how the colours have disappeared and how the picture has been restored to its original condition. You must go there once, my young friend. You will probably get an old guide in which it still says that the people of Pisa are resolved to restore the paintings; well, that has now happened. Non-Italian guide books still report as a curiosity the fact that through the wonderful qualities of the soil at Pisa the dead become skeletons in twenty-four hours. That is a good deal quicker than the speed with which guides to the city can provide information about the restorations. It will take them a long time to catch up! Perhaps by that time the Museo Nazionale in San Matteo will be crowded with visitors, too. To me it is still one of the undiscovered places, a monastery built in the thirteenth century and renovated a few hundred years later. Not many visitors go there, perhaps because it lies a little outside the beautiful centre of the city and the paintings are like those produced during the same period in Perugia and Assisi. Everything from the pre-Renaissance period really has a family resemblance; it is all a little stiff, with a good deal of gold. This is true even of the work of Fra Angelico, the good monk of Florence who used to kneel when he was painting the Madonna. The work of these primitives is somewhat Byzantine, and they are not sparing with martyrdoms. How often on a trip through northern Italy one sees St. Sebastian pierced by arrows! These medieval painters were continually occupied with man's many different ways of doing away with his fellow men. In the long run this becomes a little monotonous, like the many Madonnas, which are frequently portraits of the painter's beloved. Satiety is a continual danger, as I noticed on my first trip. The Palazzo dell' Academia delle Scienze in Turin is splendid, with its excellent museum of Egyptian antiquities and its Galleria Sabauda, where more foreign masters (Van Eyck, Memlinck, Rogier van der Weyden) hang than anywhere else in Italy. In Genoa one can spend unforgettable hours in the outstandingly well-stocked treasury of the cathedral of San Lorenzo, where you can see the cup which the Queen of Sheba is supposed to have given to King Solomon and from which Christ drank at the Last Supper. In Genoa I also visited a few palaces which Rubens wrote about between 1621 and 1627, when he was working there, and in which one can still see many paintings by Van Dyke. The expenses soon mount up; on each occasion I was relieved of 150 to 200 lire, and it is therefore just as well to be careful to visit these places when admission is free.

At any rate, after my first visit I vowed that I would see no more art for the time being. It is a sickness that soon passes away. I had promised myself a couple of excursions from Milan, as relief from too heavy a diet of art, namely to the 'Gra Car', the Gratiarum Cartusia, the Carthusian monastery of the Graces of Pavia, and to Bergamo. These are two places that no one should miss. The monastery was founded in 1396 by Gian Galazzo Visconti, one of the rulers of Milan, and it is probably the most expensive residence ever built for monks. The Viscontis and their successors, the Sforzas, hoped, through the sums that were spent on it, to do penance for their numerous sins. For centuries the artists of Lombardy lavished their best efforts on it. The monks have disappeared, but the cells in which they lived are still there. They can hardly be called cells; they are more like little houses with gardens, in which they spent the time when they were not sitting in the chapel, where they went three times a day. There is hardly a square inch to be found without some kind of artistic decoration. It is a very impressive building.

49. Florence

50. Florence: Palazzo Vecchio from the Loggia di Lanzi
51. Florence: Palazzo Vecchio, *Perseus* and *Medusa* ▶

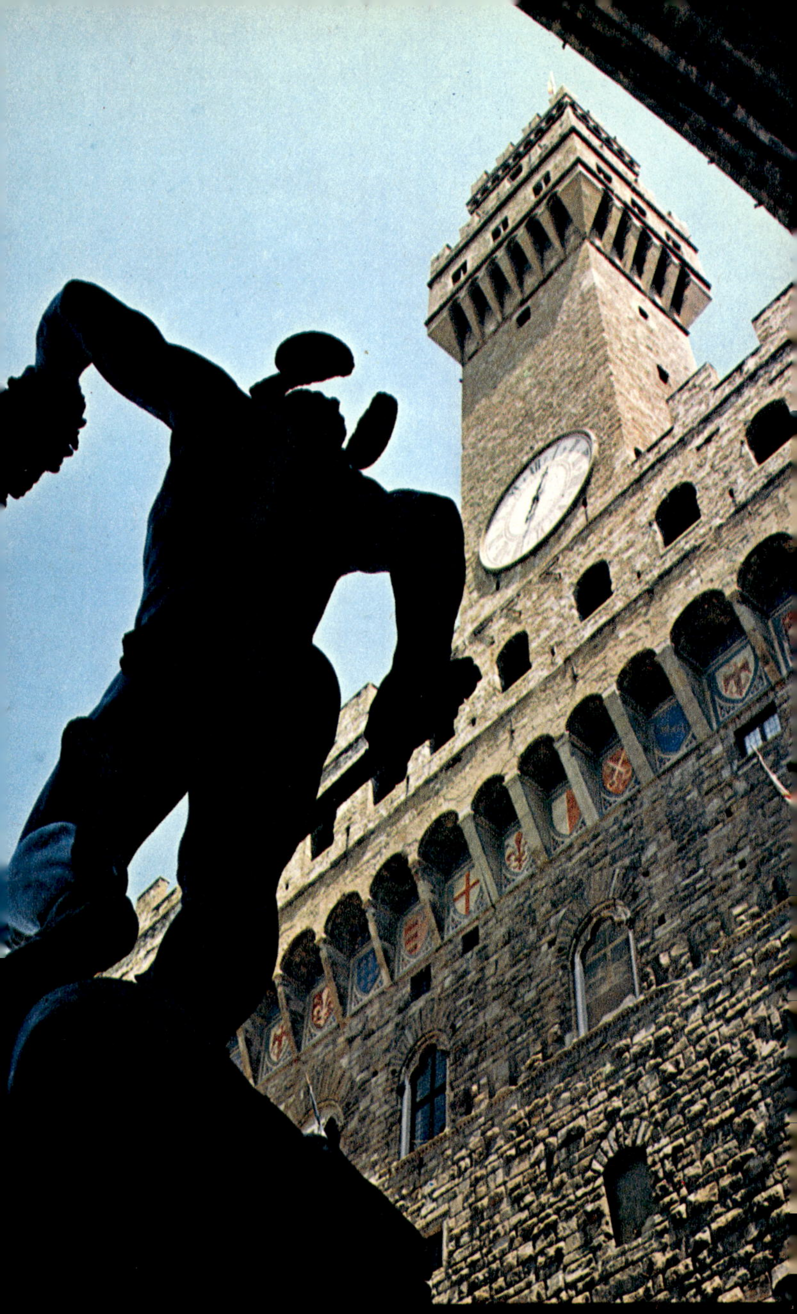

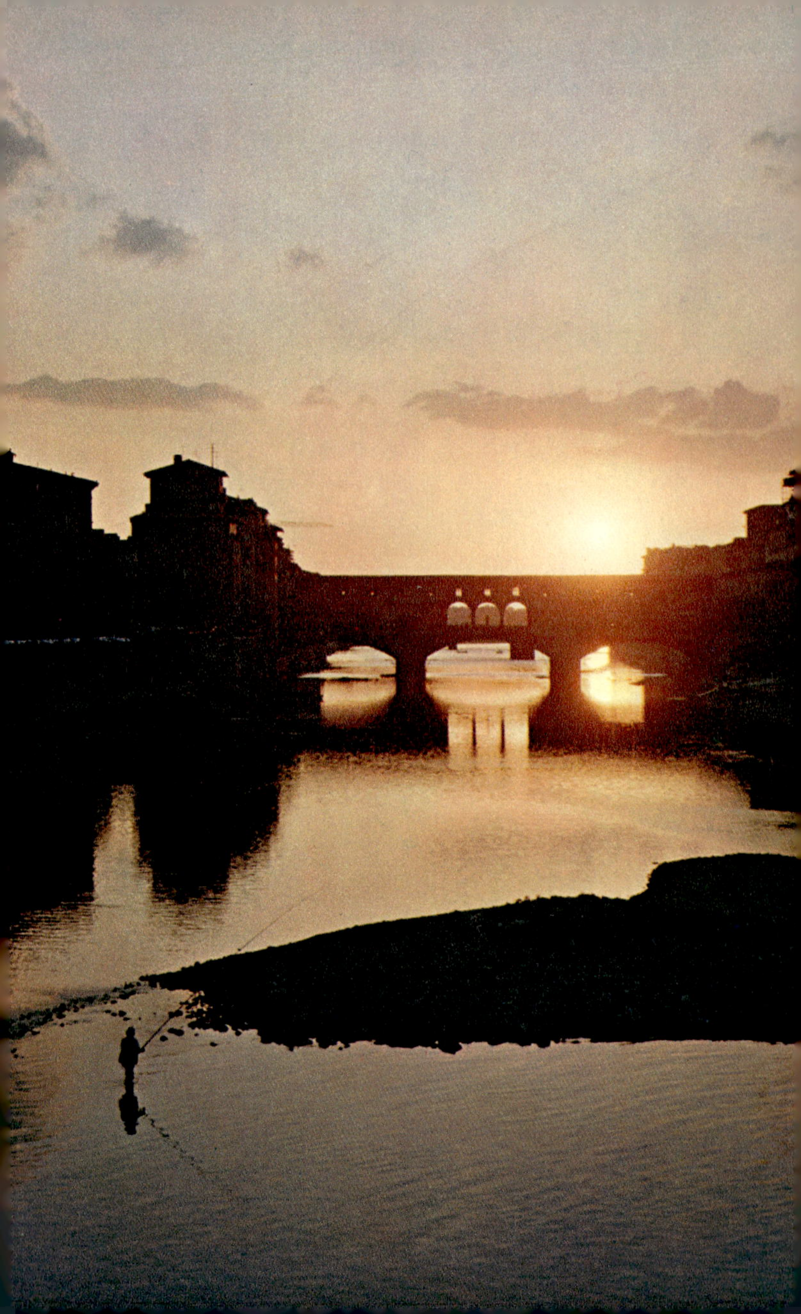

53. Florence: Baptistry, mosaic in the dome
◀ 52. Florence, Ponte Vecchio

54. Florence, San Miniato al Monte

55. Palio, Siena

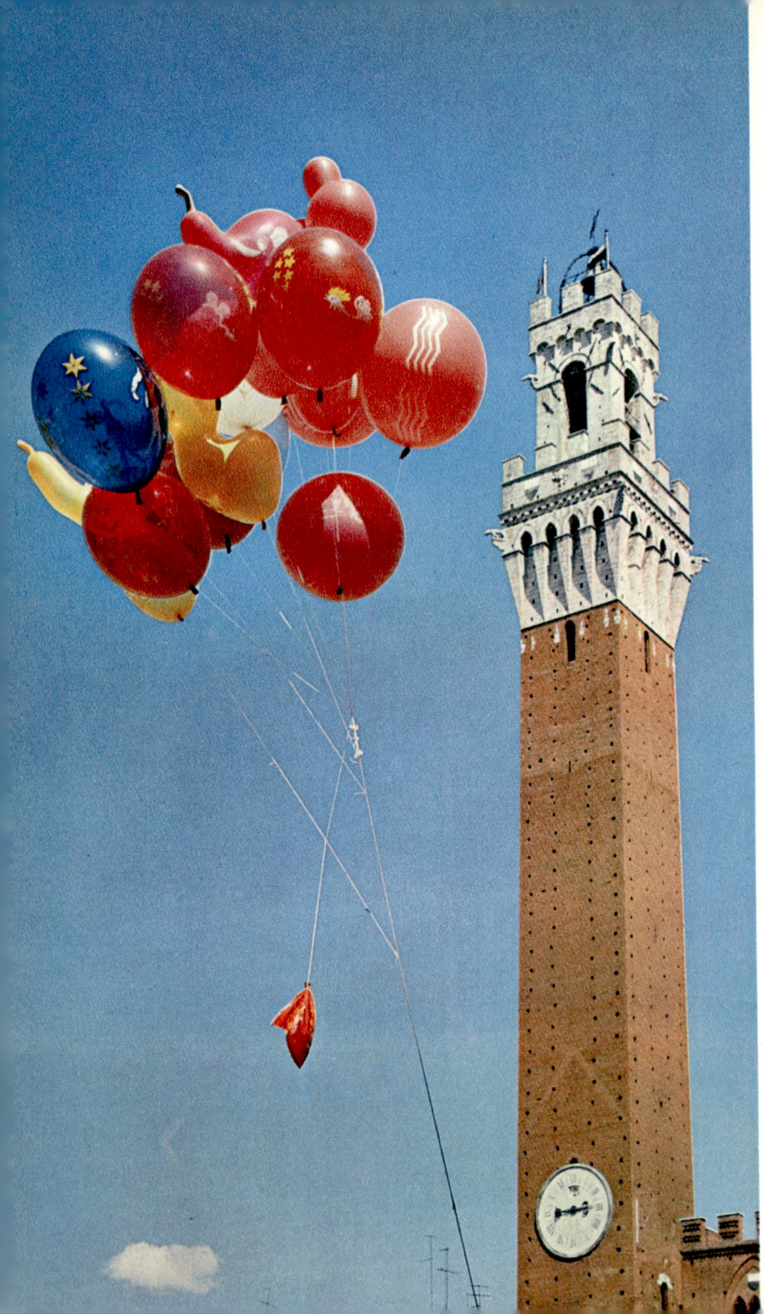

57. Palio, Siena
◀ 56. Siena: Town-hall

58. Oliena, Sardinia

59. Arbatax fisherwoman, Sardinia

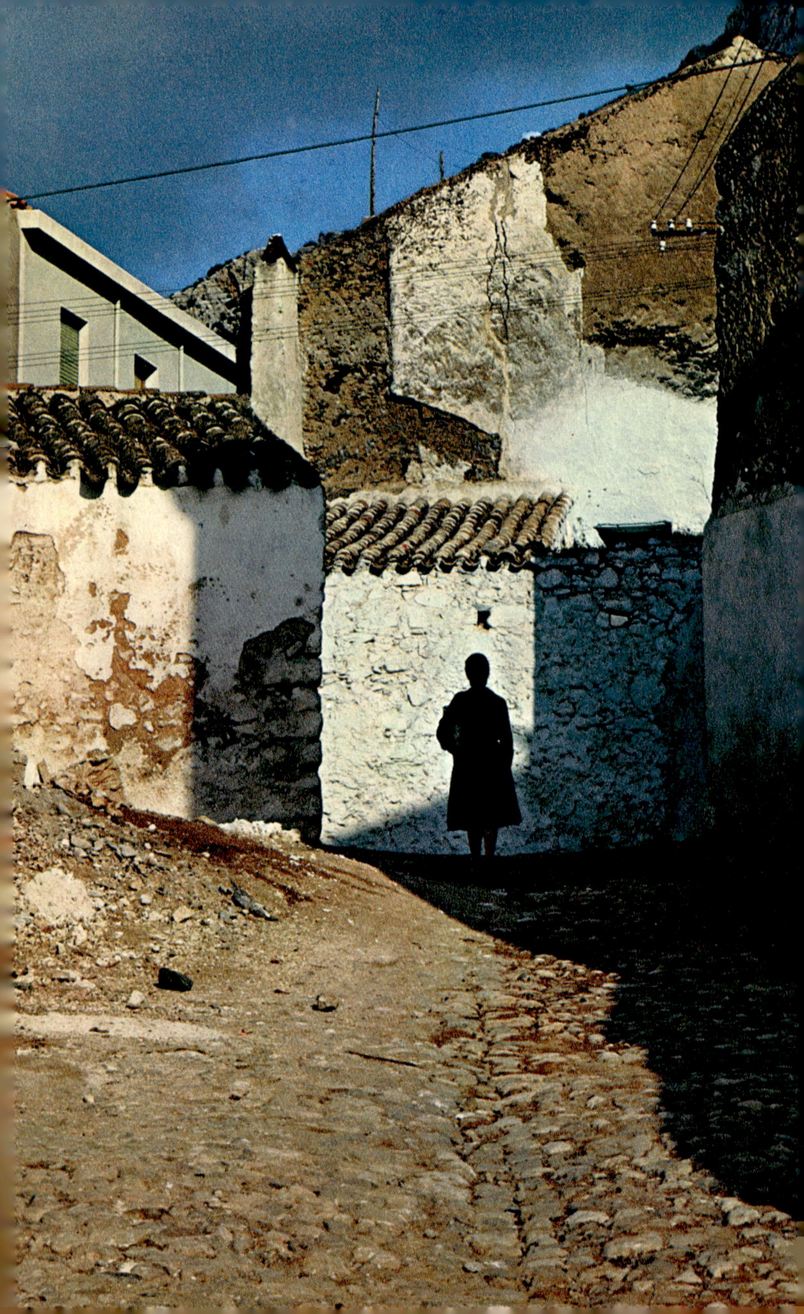

61. Oliena: farmer in local costume
◀ 60. Oliena

62. Sardinia: Tortoli

63. Near Macomer, Sardinia

64. Sardinia

Bergamo is also an impressive town. The old part, *Bergamo Alta* (high Bergamo), has remained intact. It is a microcosm of Italy — in its situation, its monuments and the view over the plain of Lombardy. "Stroll round it as if in a dream" says an admirer, "in the peace of a beautiful starry night *(una bella notte stellata)* and then go back in the morning to enjoy the dream that has then become reality." There are buildings from every century standing next to each other at random; a Romanesque cathedral by a seventeenth-century palace, a chapel dating from the early Renaissance next to a Gothic church. And they all fit in with each other. There is a book by George Mikes called *Italy for Beginners;* Bergamo is a better introduction, a complete and unforgettable one.

I really ought not to use too many superlatives, my friend, if only because you have to keep an eye on your time and you will reproach yourself for missing something. But when you return from Italy you will admit that it is difficult to find other words for what you have seen.

For a long time I avoided the Italian lakes because everyone goes to them. You will understand why they do if you drive along the western shore of Lake Garda. The road cost the lives of many who worked on it. At any rate, their names are inscribed on a board, with the remark that they died to give the tourist these unforgettable views. The Roman writers Catullus, Vergil and Pliny sang the lake's beauties, and they have had a dozen successors. Their journey along its shores was somewhat more difficult than that of the modern tourist, who can take a comfortable boat — many times a day in the season. The road from Salo, where the most beautiful part begins, to Riva, at the northern end, is 26 miles long and includes 56 bridges and 70 tunnels — so close are the mountains to the water. The hurried visitor will miss much on the way. In some cases — Salo, for example, where the inventor of the violin, Bertolotti, was born — this is of no consequence, but it would be a pity not to see, at Gardone, the house of the poet, Gabriele d' Annunzio, a man who was extravagantly fond of life and wanted to die by Lake Garda. And however great one's hurry it is essential to make time to stop at Tignale and visit the sanctuary of Madonno di Monte Castello, with its wonderful view.

That is only one of the lakes, and only one of the numerous roads which have led many a person to make a detour. This once cost me an extra day, when I had to be in Lido di Jesolo on the Adriatic by a certain date. That was on the magnificent road through the Dolomites from Bolzano to Cortina d'Ampezzo. These mountains are always changing, sometimes incredibly wild, sometimes soft and gentle. Tourists go there almost the whole year through; in the winter those who love skiing, in the summer anyone who likes mountains and walking. The distance between the two places in only 69 miles, but one does not drive straight from one to the other. The Italians have always been excellent road-builders, even long ago, when merchants travelling from Venice to Germany were able to use the mountain roads without too much difficulty. The Dolomites are known as the most beautiful range of mountains in the Alps. They sometimes look like big castles or tall towers; there are fine forests, and nowhere is the famous Alpine glow more unforgettable. When it is misty or raining in Milan the sun is often shining in the Dolomites. As always, the Italian has made the most of a favourable climate. In the valleys grapes and fruit grow in abundance, higher up many people make a good living out of the forests, and the mountains all round, frequently or always covered in snow, attract skiers. Nowhere is the hand of man to be seen more clearly on the landscape; here he has made even the heights serve his purposes. Eveywhere there are hotels to suit every purse. Even the hotel-restaurant in Trente (the church there, where the famous Council was held, is worth a visit), which gets a star in the French Michelin guide, was not too expensive — much cheaper than comparable establishments in France.

I am straying off the subject, I know, as I have so often strayed in northern Italy, though more often because of the scenery than because of restaurants. We did finally arrive in Lido di Jesolo. I must say that my children were absolutely delighted with it. It lies about nineteen miles to the east of Venice. Before the war it did not exist and even now few people live there in the winter. In the season it is literally deafening there. Yet it is the only place in Italy, apart from Rome, where I have spent a whole month. At that time there were, I think, 1500 juke boxes there, and this number will certainly not have decreased. But what a beach! Resorts like this are springing up all the way along the Adriatic from Trieste to Brindisi. In days gone by there were a few little seaside places between Venice and Ravenna, but they were difficult to reach. Now a splendid road runs along close to the coast, and everywhere there are new lidos, with bungalows and towering hotels. In the summer they are crowded, in the winter they are dead places, like Lido di Jesolo; in August it contains some 200,000 people, of whom about 5,000 — the real inhabitants — are left in December. Every morning when we awoke the sun was shining from a deep blue sky, until in the end I thought: "if it would only rain just once." When it finally did, it rained with a vengeance; but how refreshing it was.

We made many stops on the way. The children fell in love with Venice, but who doesn't? "You can have seen all the cities in the world," wrote Chateaubriand, "and still be surprised when you arrive in Venice." Another Frenchman, Paul de Musset, said that one can only talk about Venice with those who know it, "who sigh when they think of it and cling to their smallest memories". This is true; to quote a third Frenchman, Renan: "Venice is one of the fairest flowers that humanity has produced." All I can really say about it is that you must go there too. But I will give you two pieces of advice. In the summer operas are performed in the evening in a square close to the Fenicet theatre. I saw Puccini's *Madam Butterfly* there. In some of the palaces round the square people sat listening on thair balconies; behind them lights burned in the rooms, so that one could see how they were furnished. It is one of those memories that never leave you. Then you must also make a trip through the islands; it will take an afternoon. After it you will always want to go back to Torcello. Once it was a town of 20,000 inhabitants; now it is quite a small village, but there are still two old churches. There is a mosaic of the Last Judgement and one of the Madonna. For that reason alone I should like to spend a considerable time on Torcello. During the month that we were at Lido di Jesolo we also went several times to Verona. What drew us at that time were the opera performances in the old Roman arena, the biggest after the Colosseum in Rome. We saw Verdi's *Aida*. In order to get cheap seats we had to be in the arena two hours before the performance began. They were not wasted hours. The spectators were almost all Italians, and they enjoyed themselves immensely. The audience was as interesting as what happened on the stage, and that itself was outstanding.

Verona cannot be seen in a few hours. It is a charming city from which the visitor cannot tear himself away. It is sad to have to leave the Piazza delle Erbe (the square of herbs), once a Roman forum where chariot races were held and now one of the most colourful markets in Italy. It is supposed to be untrue that Romeo courted Juliet in the square that is now pointed out to you, but it is a beautiful spot and this drama of love could well have been played out there. Everything is good in Verona: its situation amid cypress-clad hills, the colour of the houses (red and ochre), the liveliness. One cannot see everything at once, but one always returns there, just as one returns to Vicenza, the city of Palladio, who was born there in 1518. He is regarded as the last great architect of the Renaissance. There are many palaces in the square, most of them built by Palladio. He had made a thorough study of Roman villas and he was fond of columns. Goethe says that he "has something godlike about him, like the form of a great poet, who weaves together truth and falsehood and so creates something that is neither, the fairylike quality of which calms and bewitches you."

You are now already pressed for time perhaps, but you must see Padua, the city — as you know — of the patron of lost objects, St. Antony, a Portuguese by birth. He died in 1231 in the neighbourhood of Padua, where he is known as *Il Santo* (The Saint). The biggest church is called the Basilica del Santo. Thousands of people make pilgrimages to it; it is always crowded, and rightly so. You may find the frescoes by Giotto in the Capella degli Scrovegni more beautiful. You will meet Giotto again later in Assisi. Personally, if I had to choose, I should rate two other places above Padua. The first is called Pomposa. The guide books seldom contain much information about it. It lies about thirty miles north of Ravenna and east of Ferrara, not far from the Adriatic coast. Pomposa is an abbey dating from the sixth century which was world-famous in the Middle Ages; one of its Benedictine monks, Guido of Arezzo, is sometimes called the father of modern music. The buildings are in excellent condition. There are the church and belltowers, which date from 1063, and magnificent decorations — symbolic animals as well as peacocks, lambs and eagles; a little green oasis, recently discovered, where the villagers come along in the evening after television to peer into the very rural hotel.

According to one of the most learned guide books, Ravenna demands a day. According to another, which tries to provide an ideal compressed trip through Italy, the grave of Dante is the only thing worth bothering about. Elsewhere I read that Ravenna is the Byzantium of the West: "the mosaics alone made the journey worth while." I am in complete agreement with this. "They are the most beautiful in Europe, more beautiful than those of Constantinople, Palermo or Venice." Once when I was at Salonica, in Greece, I fell out with a well informed lady, who made me see the mosaics in the churches of her own city. I still maintained that they came second, after those of Ravenna. End of discussion!

I must now be brief, but the photographs in his book will explain what I have no further time to put into words.

According to Renan, Florence has done more for the human spirit than any other city except Athens. It is always a festive occasion in Florence. One could stroll through the streets there for days without visiting one church or museum and without becoming bored.

The shops, and not only those on the Ponte Vecchio, the markets, the squares, the Piazza del Duomo and the Piazza della Signoria are always filled with a lively crowd, in the daytime at least, for the Florentine likes a quiet evening at home. And all the time there are real festivals, such as a football match in medieval dress on the first Sunday in May, and in September the *Rificolone,* a sort of folklore regatta on the River Arno.

The tragic flooding of the same river in November, 1966 caused irreparable loss in terms of human life and art; it could not, however, destroy the spirit of Florence.

The hotels provide free of charge small books in which the events of the season are described. They are worthy little works, which repay half an hour's study, especially if one has not made the best preparations for one's trip in advance. The danger is always that one may become so buried in the books that one forgets to look at the things decribed in them.

That has sometimes happened to me in Umbria. I always want to read again St. Francis' *Canticle of the Sun,* which was written there: "Praised be thou, O Lord, by brother wind, and by light and clouds and bright sky — and everything through which thou givest support to thy creation." And I want to know where he preached to the birds, in Bergamo. Or where he sang God's praises in turn with a nightingale. One of the delights of Umbria is that there one can believe that these things really happenend and perhaps could happen again. But don't forget to keep your eyes open on the way to his town.

This region is also the land of Piero della Francesca, whom connoisseurs consider the greatest painter of Italy. He painted frescoes in the church of St. Francis at Arezzo. There must have been a profound difference between the characters of Francis and Piero, the former enthusiastic and full of jubilation, the latter — in his works, at any rate — cool and very restrained. Yet they saw the same landscapes and the same towns — Lake Trasimene and high Cortona, where the streets are so steep that they often change into steps. What they were probably not interested in was the Etruscan tombs. It is true that interest in them has only developed fairly recently, and it is only in this century that we have obtained a good insight into Etruscan art. Cortona was an Etruscan city; so were Perugia, Chiusa, Vulci, Tarquinia and Cerveteri. They buried their dead in real treasure-chambers, which were usually big, round artificial hills of stone. The interior walls were painted, and the dead were surrounded by the articles which they had used during their lives. Few spots are so redolent of a rich past as these strange burial-places.

But the time has come to leave Italy for home. You will have continually made notes about the places which you want to visit again later. In Siena you will have resolved to return when the *Palio*, the famous horse-race, is held on the 2nd July and the 16th August, a competition between the seventeen districts of the city.

If I were returning home through France, I should take road along the Mediterranean. From Siena you can drive via San Gimignano. It was built in the fourteenth century and has changed little. Of the 62 old towers with which the rich families protected themselves against each other in days gone by, 13 are still standing. They make an overwhelming impression, like a town full of skyscrapers. For this reason San Gimignano is called the Manhattan of Tuscany. The road along the Mediterranean to Ventimiglia is enchanting. Often it is the view of the sea itself which is delightful, but the towns and villages are an almost constant pleasure. You have often heard of them; their names alone are poetic — Santa Margherita, Portofino, Alassio and many others. When you presently cross the French frontier at Mentone the nostalgia for Italy will begin at once. It has already happened to hundred of thousands of people and you will not be the last.